Praying the Catechism

Praying the Catechism
Opening Your Heart to Divine Wisdom

PRAYERS AND MEDITATIONS

Louise Perrotta

CHARIS

SERVANT PUBLICATIONS
ANN ARBOR, MICHIGAN

Charis Books is an imprint of Servant Publications designed to serve Roman Catholics.

Unless otherwise noted, all Scripture quotations are from the Revised Standard Version of the Bible, © 1946, 1952, 1971 by the Division of Christian Education of the National Council of the Churches of Christ in the USA. All rights reserved.

Excerpts from the English translation of the *Catechism of the Catholic Church* for use in the United States of America. © 1994, United States Catholic Conference, Inc.-Libreria Editrice Vaticana. Used with Permission.

Excerpts from the English translation of the *Catechism of the Catholic Church: Modifications from the "Editio Typica."* © 1997, United States Catholic Conference, Inc.-Libreria Editrice Vaticana. Used with Permission.

The following excerpts by Dorothy Day are courtesy of the Dorothy Day Library on the Web at http://www.catholicworker.org/dorothyday: With paragraph 1336 of the *Catechism: From Union Square to Rome*, 160, 161, 162, 163. With paragraph 2449: "The Mystery of the Poor," *The Catholic Worker*, April 1964, 2. With paragraph 2653: "Obedience," *Ave Maria*, December 17, 1966, 23.

Published by Servant Publications
P.O. Box 8617
Ann Arbor, Michigan 48107

Cover design: Michael Andaloro. Cover photograph: Howard DeCruyenaere

00 01 02 03 10 9 8 7 6 5 4 3 2 1

Printed in the United States of America
ISBN 0-56955-207-X

LIBRARY OF CONGRESS CATALOGING-IN-PUBLICATION DATA

Perrotta, Louise.
Praying the catechism : opening your heart to divine wisdom : prayers and meditations / Louise Perrotta.
   p.   cm.
Includes index
ISBN 1-56955-207-X (alk. paper)
1. Catholic Church. Catechismus Ecclesiae Catholicae. 2. Catholic Church—Prayerbooks and devotions—English. I. Title.
BX1959.5.P47 2000
238'.2—dc21   00-056126

This is dedicated to Cardinal Bernard Law,
who suggested the idea of the *Catechism*,
and to Heidi Hess Saxton,
who suggested this book.

CONTENTS

INTRODUCTION

I admit it: this book wasn't my idea.

What exactly I said when it was first proposed to me I don't remember. What I thought—and what I also heard later from a few of the people to whom I mentioned the project—went something like this: "*Pray* the *Catechism*? Doesn't that sound kind of dry—like praying an instruction manual?"

Well, now that I have prayed my way through the *Catechism of the Catholic Church*, I have another admission: I was wrong.

Using the *Catechism* as a springboard for personal prayer is anything but dry for at least two reasons. First, the truths of the faith which the *Catechism* explains are exciting and become even more so as they are pondered and prayed. They revolve around God's loving purposes for the human race—a "plan of sheer goodness" which invites us to become God's "adopted children and thus heirs of his blessed life" (*CCC*, 1).

As presented in the *Catechism*, this teaching also holds our interest because it addresses modern needs. It aims "to illumine with the light of faith the new situations and problems which had not yet emerged in the past," as Pope John Paul II wrote in the 1992 Apostolic Constitution that precedes the *Catechism* text.[1] Like the savvy Gospel householder "who brings

out of his treasure what is new and what is old"
(Matthew 13:52), the *Catechism* reveals the faith as
"always the same yet the source of ever new light."

The second reason why praying the *Catechism* is
fruitful and not dry and sterile has to do with the
Holy Spirit, master teacher of prayer. "The Spirit
helps us in our weakness; for we do not know how to
pray as we ought" (Romans 8:26). This is true when-
ever we seek to pray. But if the Spirit stands ready to
help us turn to God with even the smallest of our
needs and concerns, how eager he must be to assist us
in contemplating the deep truths of our faith! Just
imagine how you'd react if one of your children—or
a niece, nephew, godchild, or grandchild—asked to
be taken to Mass instead of a movie. Wouldn't you
move heaven and earth to answer that request?
Imperfect as it is, the analogy should at least encourage us to approach the Holy Spirit with confidence as
we seek to pray the *Catechism*.

Praying the Catechism follows the *Catechism*'s
structure, which rests on four basic pillars: the profession of faith, with its focus on the Creed; the liturgy,
especially the sacraments; the life of faith, in which
right conduct is guided by the Ten Commandments;
and prayer, with emphasis on the Our Father.

Each of the 160 prayers or meditations in this book
takes a short excerpt from the *Catechism* as its starting

point. For easy reference, every excerpt is identified by its *Catechism* paragraph number (these appear in parentheses after each citation). Except for Scripture references, which have been inserted into the *Catechism* excerpts, material that appears in footnotes in the *Catechism* has been placed in a "Notes" section in the back of this book.

Like the *Catechism*, which illustrates and reinforces its points by drawing on Scripture, as well as a variety of ecclesiastical documents and the writings of Church Fathers and other saints, *Praying the Catechism* owes its prayers and meditations to many sources. Many have been inspired or taken directly from Scripture. Some are from Church Fathers, some from saints, some from contemporary spiritual writers; some are original. For maximum benefit, use this book with your Bible and your *Catechism* close at hand. You may feel a desire to read through the full version of a scripture passage, for example. Or you might want to consult your *Catechism* for the full text or the context of the paragraph from which a particular excerpt is taken.

Why Pray the *Catechism*?

For balance. Guided by the *Catechism*, our prayer can become less scattershot, better grounded in the basics of the faith, more in sync with the Church, less self-centered and more truly "catholic"—that is, universal—in its scope.

For knowledge. The *Catechism* provides solid content for prayer, and on many points where our thinking may be fuzzy or otherwise deficient. Not only that: as it feeds the intellect, prayerful reflection on basic spiritual truths converts the heart. As St. John Damascene remarked of prayer in general, it is ... "the raising of one's mind and heart to God." ...(*CCC* 2559)[2]

For love. With some relationships, the saying is true: "Familiarity breeds contempt"—the more you know, the less you see to appreciate. Emphatically not so with God! In fact, this is the only relationship that will never disappoint us, will never seem to hold more promise than it can deliver.

To know God is to love him. To know him better is to love him more—and to express that love in ever deepening prayer. Let us open ourselves to love by praying the *Catechism!*

Louise Perrotta
Feast of the Presentation of the Lord, 2000

PART ONE
Lord, We Believe

To pray Part One of the *Catechism*, "The Profession of Faith," is to ponder the mysteries that underlie all of Christian prayer. Who is God? Why would an awesome, self-sufficient Creator seek a personal relationship with *me*? How does his desire for us awaken our desire for him? Meditating on God's loving initiatives, on the disproportion between who we are and what God has done for us, can help us to grow in that humility which is the very foundation of prayer.

Additionally, this first quarter of the *Catechism* underlines the importance of searching for God and responding in obedient faith to the truth he reveals. This is the perennial dynamic of prayer, and both the spiritual beginner and the seasoned follower of Christ will benefit from keeping it in mind.

Especially prominent here—it provides the organizing framework for examining the different aspects of God's revelation to us—is one particular prayer, the Creed. As we pray our way through the articles of faith it presents, may the Creed become for us a wellspring of thanks and praise for God's marvelous plan of salvation:

This Creed is the spiritual seal,
our heart's meditation and an
ever-present guardian;
it is, unquestionably,
the treasure of our soul.

St. Ambrose[3]

O God, we long to know your love.

The desire for God is written in the human heart....
(CCC 27)

Prayer for Today:
We find no perfect contentment here; nothing this world offers can satisfy our desires. The mind ever wants to know more; the will never comes to an end of its search for goodness to love. Surely we can recognize that it is not for this world we were made! A supreme good attracts us, some infinite craftsman who has fashioned us with an endless longing for knowledge, with a hunger for good that knows no appeasement. That is why we must turn and reach out towards God—creatures of whose fashioning we are—and seek for union with his goodness.

St. Francis de Sales

Loving Creator, how slow we are to understand ourselves—to see and marvel that we were created for nothing less than union with you! How often we misinterpret our desires and go looking for happiness and fulfillment in all the wrong places. Help us to understand our heart's deepest longings, for it is your face we seek, your voice we strain to hear, your love we long for. Awaken our desire for you, dear God, and draw us into your loving embrace.

Let all creation proclaim and praise the living God!

"Question the beauty of the earth, question the beauty of the sea, question the beauty of the air distending and diffusing itself, question the beauty of the sky... question all these realities. All respond: 'See, we are beautiful.' Their beauty is a profession."

Saint Augustine (CCC 32)[4]

Prayer for Today: Magnificent God, how glorious is the work of your hands! Every star and flower, every sunrise and mountain range speaks of your wisdom and goodness and power. In the things you have created, we glimpse something of your beauty, and we stand amazed. Forgive us for not always being good stewards of your handiwork. Forgive us for the times when we take it for granted or ignore its witness to you.

"The heavens are telling the glory of God; and the firmament proclaims his handiwork" (Psalm 19:1). From every corner of the universe, your creation speaks of you and offers its song of praise. Show us how to add our voices to that unending chorus today.

Something about us reveals something about God.

All creatures bear a certain resemblance to God, most especially man, created in the image and likeness of God. *(CCC 41)*

Prayer for Today: What incredible dignity you conferred on us human beings, Lord, when you made us in your image. Not only did you create us: you created us to know and love you! Not only did you give us life: you offered us a share in your life!

Today, Lord, help me to recognize my unique place in your creation and to offer you a grateful response of faithful love. May I treat myself with respect—doing nothing to tarnish your likeness in me, doing all I can so that it shines more brightly. May I treat other people with respect, too, especially those I find most difficult and irritating. No matter how dimly I perceive your image in them, you love them and are calling them to yourself.

Marvel at the mystery:
God's love for us, God's life in us.

"It pleased God, in his goodness and wisdom, to reveal himself and to make known the mystery of his will. His will was that men should have access to the Father, through Christ, the Word made flesh, in the Holy Spirit, and thus become sharers in the divine nature."

(*CCC* 51)[5]

Reflection for Today: What an astonishing plan God devised to save us! What unprecedented mercy our Creator extends to his fallen creatures! "For God so loved the world that he gave his only Son, that whoever believes in him should not perish but have eternal life" (John 3:16).

Such wondrous love should pierce us to the heart. It should move us to surrender ourselves totally to God. But does it? Or have we become somewhat dulled to the radical meaning of the incarnation?

O depth of love! What heart could keep from breaking at the sight of your greatness descending to the lowliness of our humanity?... And why? For love! You, God, became human and we have been made divine!

St. Catherine of Siena

Over and over, God loves and saves.

After the unity of the human race was shattered by sin
God at once sought to save humanity part by part.

(*CCC* 56)

Prayer for Today: *Thank you, God ...*
For not giving up on the human race
    after our first parents' sin,
For rescuing Noah and his family
    and making a covenant with him,
For calling Abraham to be
    the father of your chosen people,
For saving and teaching them through Moses,
For your prophets, whose calls to repentance
    prepared the way for your Son,
For Sarah, Rebecca, Rachel,
    and all the holy men and women
    who kept alive the hope of your salvation,
For all those who hailed the light of Christ's dawning:
    shepherds and magi,
    Anna and Simeon,
    Elizabeth and Zechariah,
    Joseph, and John the Baptist,
    and especially for Mary,
    privileged instrument of your loving plan.
For all this, O God, of second chances and new
    beginnings,
and for your unfailing patience with us when we stumble,
we give you thanks and praise.

Jesus is the answer.

Christ, the Son of God made man, is the Father's one, perfect, and unsurpassable Word. In him he has said everything.... (*CCC* 65)

Prayer for Today: Jesus, you are the eternal Word of God who comes to meet me in the Scriptures. Jesus, you are the Word made flesh, the bread of life, who nourishes me in the Eucharist. In you, Lord, I have everything.

Jesus is the Word to be spoken.
Jesus is the truth to be told.
Jesus is the way to be walked.
Jesus is the light to be lit.
Jesus is the life to be lived.
Jesus is the love to be loved....
Jesus is my life.
Jesus is my only love.
Jesus is my all in all.
Jesus is my everything.

from a prayer by Mother Teresa

When Scripture is difficult to understand.

"But above all it's the Gospels that occupy my mind when I'm at prayer; my poor soul has so many needs, and yet this is the one thing needful. I'm always finding fresh lights there, hidden and enthralling meanings."

St. Thérèse of Lisieux (*CCC* 127)[6]

Prayer for Today: Lord Jesus, I'm no St. Thérèse. Some days even the Gospels seem like a closed book to me. You seem far away, and I feel discouraged about being so slow to understand and believe.

But then I remember what you did for those two disciples on the road to Emmaus (see Luke 24:13-35). They didn't understand, either. They were depressed and discouraged, afraid and doubtful. But all that changed as you broke bread with them and opened the Scriptures for them. You set their hearts afire.

Please, Lord, do the same for *this* dense disciple! Kindle in me the fire of faith, the fire of your love.

Faith takes risks.

To obey ... in faith is to submit freely to the word that has been heard, because its truth is guaranteed by God, who is Truth itself. (*CCC* 144)

Reflection for Today: Obedient faith takes God at his word—even when acting on that word feels inconvenient or risky. Think about Abraham, "the father of all who believe" (Romans 4:11). Read about his response of faith (Hebrews 11:8-12, 17-19). Consider Mary, the most perfect example of the faithful disciple, whose faith journey began when she accepted God's invitation to a unique pregnancy (see Luke 1:26-38).

In your own life, where is God especially calling you to obey his word in faith? Are you willing to exercise your faith by changing something about how you live? by taking necessary risks?

Make a brief examination of conscience occasionally on this one point: "Do I ever do anything in my life which I should not have done if Christ had not come on earth?"... If your life rolls on, from morning till night, with nothing unforeseen, if everything about you ... can be explained in human terms, then Christianity has not penetrated you to your very depths.

Cardinal Leon Joseph Suenens

What you have freely received, freely give.

... faith is not an isolated act.... You have not given yourself faith as you have not given yourself life. The believer has received faith from others and should hand it on to others. (*CCC* 166)

Prayer for Today: How can I ever thank you, Jesus, for your Church—that great chain of believers through whom I received faith?

I think of your apostles, who spoke your word with authority; of your martyrs, who defended it with their lives; of your teachers and thinkers, who transmitted it faithfully, unfolding its meaning under the Spirit's guidance.

I remember the people who first taught me about you, and those from whom I'm learning now—parents and other family members, godparents, nuns and priests, teachers, spiritual writers and guides, friends in heaven and on earth.

I will declare your goodness! I will take my place in that great chain of believers. By what I say and how I live, I will hand on to others the faith I have received.

I love you, Jesus, and I want everyone to know and love you too. Show me what to do.

You are great beyond all imagining, O God!

Even when he reveals himself, God remains a mystery beyond words: "If you understood him, it would not be God."

St. Augustine (CCC 230)[7]

Prayer for Today: Eternal Trinity, however much I may come to know you, I humbly acknowledge that I can never fully understand you. Help me to identify and reject ways of thinking and acting that are really my attempts to fashion a god I can control. Forgive me for every time I've tried to manipulate you.

O the depth of the riches and wisdom and knowledge of God! How unsearchable are his judgments and how inscrutable his ways!
"For who has known the mind of the Lord,
or who has been his counselor?"
"Or who has given a gift to him
that he might be repaid?"
For from him and through him and to him are all things. To him be glory forever. Amen.

ROMANS 11:33-36

Adore God at the center.

The mystery of the Most Holy Trinity is the central mystery of Christian faith and life. It is the mystery of God in himself. (*CCC* 234)

Prayer for Today:

O my God, Trinity Whom I adore,
help me to forget myself entirely
that I may be established in You
as still and as peaceful
as if my soul were already in eternity.

May nothing trouble my peace
or make me leave You,
O my unchanging One,
but may each minute
carry me further
into the depths of Your Mystery.

Give peace to my soul,
make it Your heaven,
Your beloved dwelling
and Your resting place.

May I never leave You there alone
but be wholly present,
my faith wholly vigilant,
wholly adoring,
and wholly surrendered to Your creative Action.

Blessed Elizabeth of the Trinity

In everything God works for good.

We firmly believe that God is master of the world and of its history. But the ways of his providence are often unknown to us.   (*CCC* 314)

Reflection for Today: What can we do when disasters, world events and personal trials make it hard to trust that God is in control, working out his loving plan of salvation (see Romans 8:28)? Listen to the words of St. Jane de Chantal ...

For this there is no remedy except to stir up our faith often that God is present everywhere and that nothing happens in the world unless it is ordained by his divine providence....

Persons who are attentive to this truth will never be disturbed. "Well," they may say, "I know that God is present with me, that he is more in me than myself. I know that he governs all things and that his eye watches over all. I know that nothing happens in heaven or earth unless he ordains or permits it. Therefore, if the waters of the lake rise up in a flood, ... I know that God is present with me and that he permits this for some reason which it belongs to his providence to know. Why, then, should I be troubled?"

O God, you rule the waves, the sky, and the earth.... In silence of spirit, I adore and revere all your hidden judgments.

St. Jane de Chantal

An angel to watch over me.

"Beside each believer stands an angel as protector and shepherd leading him to life."

St. Basil (*CCC* 336)[8]

Reflection for Today: Pope John XXIII, who had a particular devotion to his guardian angel, rejoiced that this special helper and intercessor was "an angel of paradise, no less"—a heavenly being rapt in ecstasy before the face of God. But the joyful thought was also humbling, he wrote, and an effective motivator for following Christ more perfectly:

How can I entertain certain proud thoughts, say certain words, commit certain actions, under the eyes of my Guardian Angel? And yet I have done this. O my spirit companion, pray to God for me, that I may never do, say, or think anything that could offend your most pure eyes.

What about you? Do you often think about your guardian angel? What could you do to develop a deeper friendship with this protecting guide and companion? How will you try to remember your guardian angel today?

Know your enemy, know your defense.

Scripture witnesses to the disastrous influence of the one Jesus calls "a murderer from the beginning" (Jn 8:44; cf. Mt 4:1-11)....   (*CCC* 394)

Prayer for Today: The devil? I'd like to forget about him, heavenly Father. But your word exposes his activity and his wicked agenda: right from the beginning, when he tempted our first parents, he seeks to turn human hearts against you.

Help me, God, to take seriously the fact that I have an enemy who "prowls around like a roaring lion, seeking some one to devour" (1 Peter 5:8). But help me, too, not to be paralyzed with fear! Teach me to resist the devil courageously, firm in the knowledge that your Son has already won the victory. Remind me to seek your help more often through the intercession of Mary and of Michael the archangel (see Revelation 12:7).

Saint Michael the Archangel, defend us in battle.
Be our safeguard against the wickedness and snares of the devil.
May God rebuke him, we humbly pray,
and may you, O prince of the heavenly hosts,
by the divine power thrust into hell Satan and all the evil spirits
who prowl about the world seeking the ruin of souls.
                                                Amen.

Father, have your way with me.

Man, tempted by the devil, let his trust in his Creator die in his heart and, abusing his freedom, disobeyed God's command. This is what man's first sin consisted of (cf. Gen 3:1-11; Rom 5:19). *(CCC 397)*

Prayer for Today: This first sin—I see it in myself, dear Father. "My way, not yours," says my pride. "I will not serve!" or "I'll serve—but only under these conditions," say so many of my actions. Why do I so often listen to that seductive whisper: "You don't need God. You can do it yourself"?

Father, I want to reject that voice and live in friendship with you. United with Jesus, may all my thoughts, words, and actions today tell you: "Not what I want, but what you want" (Mark 14:36 NRSV).

I put myself into your hands, O Lord.
Make me what you will.
I forget myself. I divorce myself from myself.
I am dead to myself.
I will follow you.
What will you have me do?
Have your own way with me.
Whatever it may be, pleasant or painful,
I will do it.

Cardinal John Henry Newman

For freedom, thanks be to God!

As a result of original sin, human nature is weakened in its powers; subject to ignorance, suffering, and the domination of death; and inclined to sin....

(*CCC* 418)

Reflection for Today: Read the following passage slowly and reflectively. Let it lead you into a prayer of thanks and praise for Christ's victory, which brings freedom from the slavery of sin.

I do not understand my own actions. For I do not do what I want, but I do the very thing I hate.... I can will what is right, but I cannot do it. For I do not do the good I want, but the evil I do not want is what I do.....
So I find it to be a law that when I want to do right, evil lies close at hand. For I delight in the law of God, in my inmost self, but I see in my members another law at war with the law of my mind and making me captive to the law of sin which dwells in my members. Wretched man that I am! Who will deliver me from this body of death? Thanks be to God through Jesus Christ our Lord!

Romans 7:15, 18b-19, 21-25

"Who do you say I am?"

We believe and confess that Jesus of Nazareth … is the eternal Son of God made man.   (*CCC* 423)

Prayer for Today: Lord, you once asked your apostles, "Who do you say that I am?" (Matthew 16:15). But your question wasn't only for them. It was for every one of your disciples, in every age, in every part of the world. It was for me. And so, drawn by your Father, enlightened by your Spirit, united with your Church, I answer:

You are Jesus, the Savior, whose very name means "God saves."
Thank you for saving me from my sins.

You are the Christ, anointed with the Spirit as priest, prophet, and king.
Thank you for inviting me into your kingdom and incorporating me into the People of God.

You are the Son of God, one in being with the Father: you are God.
Thank you for revealing the Father and for making me his child.

You are Lord, divine ruler of the world.
My Lord and my God, I adore you.

And the Word became flesh.

Why did the Word become flesh? (*CCC* 456)

Reflection for Today: Sometimes you can find raw material for prayer even in the headings of the *Catechism*—this one, for example. The *Catechism* offers four answers to the question (presented below). But before moving your eyes down this page, take a few moments to consider what reasons *you* can think of.

God could undoubtedly have saved us in a number of ways. Why might he have chosen this one? Why the Incarnation? Jot down your thoughts, if you have time. Then choose one of the following points to reflect on, looking up at least one of the related Bible verses.

The Word became flesh so that:

- we could be saved from sin and restored to friendship with God (see 1 John 4:10; 4:14; 3:5).
- we could come to know God's love (see 1 John 4:9; John 3:16).
- we could have a model of holiness—someone to study and follow (see Matthew 11:29; John 15:12).
- we could share in God's own nature (see 2 Peter 1:4).

Blessed are you among women.

"The knot of Eve's disobedience was untied by Mary's obedience: what the virgin Eve bound through her disbelief, Mary loosened by her faith."

St. Irenaeus (CCC 494)[9]

Prayer for Today: Holy Mary—ever-Virgin and Mother of God—we honor you for saying yes to the divine plan of salvation. Pray for us.

The Angelus

The angel of the Lord declared unto Mary,
And she conceived of the Holy Spirit.
Hail Mary, full of grace....

Behold the handmaid of the Lord,
Let it be done to me according to your word.
Hail Mary....

And the Word was made flesh,
And dwelt among us.
Hail Mary....

Pray for us, O holy Mother of God,
that we may be worthy of the promises of Christ.
Let us pray.
Pour forth, we beseech you, O Lord, your grace into our hearts, that we, to whom the Incarnation of Christ, your Son, was made known by the message of an angel, may be brought by his passion and cross to the glory of his Resurrection, through the same Christ our Lord, Amen.

What he commands, he makes possible.

In all of his life Jesus presents himself as *our model*.
(*CCC* 520)

Prayer for Today: "Be imitators of God, as beloved children. And walk in love, as Christ loved us and gave himself up for us" (Ephesians 5:1-2).

How lost we would be, Lord Jesus, without your example to guide us! All the episodes of your earthly life are so rich with practical meaning for our own. As we ponder them in the Gospels, the rosary, the stations of the cross, the feasts of the Church year, each one shows us how to live and invites us to imitate you more closely.

But what an impossible mission it would be, Lord, if we had to imitate you on our own strength, like a self-help program! How graciously you walk beside us, and move inside us, transforming us to become like you. As we die to ourselves, you are revealed in us.

But we have this treasure in earthen vessels.... For while we live we are always being given up to death for Jesus' sake, so that the life of Jesus may be manifested in our mortal flesh.

2 CORINTHIANS 4:7, 11

Knowing we are loved.

By giving up his own Son for our sins, God manifests that his plan for us is one of benevolent love, prior to any merit on our part…. (*CCC* 604)

Reflection for Today: Sometimes in the ordinariness and turmoil of daily life, it's easy to lose sight of basic realities—like the fact that we are precious to our Maker. Dorothy Day once described how this reality was impressed on her one lonely evening when she was far from home:

And suddenly the thought came to me of my importance as a daughter of God, daughter of a King, and I felt a sureness of God's love…. God so loved me that he gave His only begotten Son. "If a mother will forget her children, never will I forget thee" [Isaiah 49:15]. Such tenderness. And with such complete ingratitude we forget the Father and his love!

Dorothy Day

O God of loving kindness, let me no longer do you the injustice of not acknowledging your love for me. No matter what this day brings, let me live it in the secure knowledge of your love. Amen.

Rising, you restored our life.

Christ is risen from the dead!
Dying, he conquered death;
To the dead, he has given life.
Byzantine Liturgy, Troparion of Easter (*CCC* 638)

Reflection for Today: St. Melito of Sardis, a second-century bishop, portrays the resurrected Christ proclaiming this message of triumphant victory over the powers of darkness:

Who will contend with me? Let him confront me. I have freed the condemned, brought the dead back to life, raised men from their graves. Who has anything to say against me? I am the Christ. I have destroyed death, triumphed over the enemy, trampled hell underfoot, bound the strong one, and taken mankind up to the heights of heaven. I am the Christ.

Come then, all you nations. Receive forgiveness for the sins that defile you. I am your forgiveness. I am the Passover that brings salvation. I am the Lamb slain for you. I am your ransom, your life, your resurrection, your light. I am your salvation and your king. I will bring you to the heights of heaven. With my own right hand I will raise you up, and I will show you the eternal Father.

St. Melito of Sardis

You are seated at the Father's right hand.

Jesus Christ, having entered the sanctuary of heaven once and for all, intercedes constantly for us as the mediator who assures us of the permanent outpouring of the Holy Spirit. (*CCC* 667)

Prayer for Today:
> Christ, ascended into heaven,
> You bear the wounds
> of the whole world
> in Your hands and feet
> and in Your heart.
>
> They plead for us,
> shining like stars
> before the secret face
> of God.

from a prayer by Caryll Houselander

Since then we have a great high priest who has passed through the heavens, Jesus, the Son of God, let us hold fast our confession.... Let us then with confidence draw near to the throne of grace, that we may receive mercy and find grace to help in time of need.

HEBREWS 4:14, 16

"You did it to me."

On the last day Jesus will say: "Truly I say to you, as you did it to one of the least of these my brethren, you did it to me" (Mt 25:40).   (*CCC* 678)

Prayer for Today:
O Jesus, you whose presence is hidden behind so many distressing disguises of human suffering and weakness, grant that I may recognize you and lovingly serve you, especially in those people whose disguises distress me the most. (*Here take a few minutes to think of those people and offer them to God.*)

Lord, you told St. Catherine of Siena:

"I have placed you among your neighbors so that you can do for them what you cannot do for me—that is, so that you may love them without any expectation of thanks or profit."

You tell me the same thing about the people I've just brought before you. Today, dear Jesus, enable me to love you in them. Amen.

Come, Holy Spirit!

... to be in touch with Christ, we must first have been touched by the Holy Spirit. He comes to meet us and kindles faith in us. (*CCC* 683)

Prayer for Today: O Spirit of God, you are sent by the Father to awaken our faith and to help us profess that Jesus is Lord (see 1 Corinthians 12:3). We welcome you and open ourselves to you!

Come, Holy Spirit, fill the hearts of your faithful, and enkindle in them the fire of your love.

Send forth your Spirit and they shall be created, And you shall renew the face of the earth.

Let us pray.
O God, who did instruct the hearts of the faithful by the light of the Holy Spirit, grant that by that same Holy Spirit we may be always truly wise and ever rejoice in his consolation. Through Christ our Lord. Amen.

On fire with the Spirit.

In the form of tongues "as of fire," the Holy Spirit rests on the disciples on the morning of Pentecost and fills them with himself (Acts 2:3-4).   (*CCC* 696)

Prayer for Today: *Imagine yourself waiting and praying in the upper room with Mary and the disciples. Pray along with them as they ask Jesus to fulfill his promise and send his Holy Spirit. Then ask the Spirit to let his fire fall afresh on you today.*

O living Flame of God, John the Baptist spoke of you when he said that Jesus would baptize us "with the Holy Spirit and with fire" (Luke 3:16). With great longing and a sense of deep need, I open myself to your transforming power. Come, Holy Spirit! Burn every evil from my heart and my mind. Transform my lukewarm love into burning zeal and ardent devotion.

Come, Holy Spirit, come O Lord who are love, fill my heart, for alas! it is empty of anything good. Set me on fire, that I may love you. Enlighten me, that I may know you. Attract me, that I may delight in you.

St. Gertrude

A prayer for end times.

By his coming, which never ceases, the Holy Spirit causes the world to enter into the "last days," the time of the Church, the Kingdom already inherited though not yet consummated. (*CCC* 732)

Prayer for Today: Holy Spirit, you whose coming never ceases, come and help your people to develop an authentic "end times" mentality. Keep us from doomsday pessimism, fretful worrying, and idle speculation about the timing of Judgment Day. Guard us from indifference and skepticism about Jesus' return in glory. May we never lose faith when the signs of your kingdom seem faint! May we always rejoice to be members of your holy Church, playing our part faithfully so that as many people as possible may enter in.

For you yourselves know well that the day of the Lord will come like a thief in the night.... So then let us not sleep, as others do.... Let us be sober, and put on the breastplate of faith and love, and for a helmet the hope of salvation. For God has not destined us for wrath, but to obtain salvation through our Lord Jesus Christ, who died for us.

1 THESSALONIANS 5:2, 6, 8-9

Heart of Jesus, birthplace of the Church.

As Eve was formed from the sleeping Adam's side, so the Church was born from the pierced heart of Christ hanging dead on the cross.   (*CCC* 766)[10]

Prayer for Today:
O Divine Redeemer, who loved the Church and gave yourself up for her,... let your holy Face shine upon her! May your Church, one in your love, holy in sharing your very holiness, still be, for the world today, the vessel of salvation for men, the center of unity for all hearts, inspiring holy resolutions for a general and stirring renewal. May her children, no longer divided, and forsaking all unworthiness, do her honor always and everywhere, so that those who do not yet belong to her may consider her and find you, the way, the truth and the life, and in you be brought back to the Father in the unity of the Holy Spirit!

Pope Paul VI

The Church is one with Christ.

"Marvel and rejoice: we have become Christ. For if he is the head, we are the members; he and we together are the whole man...."

St. Augustine (CCC 795)[11]

Reflection for Today: Being part of Christ's Body is an awesome reality that offers many facets for reflection. Today take a few minutes to ponder this one, from Jean-Baptist Chautard's spiritual classic, *The Soul of the Apostolate:*

What love for you this thought kindles in my heart, O Holy Church of God! I am one of your members! I am a member of Christ! What love for all Christians this thought gives me, since I see that they are my brothers and sisters and that we are one in Christ! What love for my divine Head, Jesus Christ!

Nothing that has to do with you can leave me indifferent. I am sad when I see you persecuted, full of rejoicing at the news of your conquests and triumphs.

What joy to think that in sanctifying myself I am also increasing your beauty and working for the sanctification of all the children of the Church, my brothers and sisters, and even for the salvation of the whole human family!

Jean-Baptist Chautard

What have I done with my gifts?

Whether extraordinary or simple and humble, charisms are graces of the Holy Spirit which directly or indirectly benefit the Church.... (*CCC* 799)

Reflection for Today: In every age the Holy Spirit blesses his people with a rich assortment of gifts for building up the Church and continuing Christ's mission on earth. "To each is given the manifestation of the Spirit for the common good," Scripture tells me (1 Corinthians 12:7). And so I ask myself, "What have I done with the gifts God has given me?"

Do I know what they are?
Am I grateful for them, or do I long restlessly for others?
Am I using them to serve people?
Have I buried my gifts—out of laziness? fear of failure? for some other reason?

Holy Spirit, I don't want to squander and overlook your gifts any more. I want to take my place of service in the Church. Show me practical ways to bring Christ's new life and mercy to the people in my life. Open my eyes to their needs and to my own abilities. Open my heart to that deep love of you which is the heart of real service.

Make us one, Lord.

Christ always gives his Church the gift of unity, but the Church must always pray and work to maintain, reinforce, and perfect the unity that Christ wills for her.

(*CCC* 820)

Prayer for Today: Lord, we come to you in sorrow over the divisions that separate your people. We mourn because your Body is broken by disagreements and lack of love. We grieve to see your name held in dishonor because of those who bear it.

Forgive us, Lord. Pardon us for the ways in which we have contributed to this scandal of disunity. Give us strength, courage, and vision to cooperate with your renewing plan.

Unite your people, Lord. Make your Body whole. Realize in us the prayer you offered to the Father just before you sacrificed your life for us: "that they may all be one. As you, Father, are in me and I am in you, may they also be one in us, so that the world may believe that you have sent me."

JOHN 17:21, NRSV

Called to be saints.

"... all the faithful, whatever their condition or state—though each in his own way—are called by the Lord to that perfection of sanctity by which the Father himself is perfect."   (*CCC* 825)[12]

Prayer for Today: Holy? Who, me? I'm not the type, Lord. I don't have that pious personality. I can't imagine myself working miracles or enduring great suffering for your sake. My prayer life is sporadic and unexciting. I'm not even a nice person all the time. Just ask my family....

But, Lord, I hear you calling... "Follow me." And so, I follow, even in my weakness. For I know that, with you, nothing is impossible!

There is another definition of what a saint is: One who, with the object of pleasing God, does his ordinary duties extraordinarily well. Such a life may be lived out without a single wonder in it, arouse little notice, be soon forgotten, and yet be the life of one of God's dearest friends....

Every person that is born is called to be a saint. Take it as most certain that you—no matter how unfitted your life may seem for holiness—are being given grace sufficient, if corresponded to, to bring you to sanctity.

Frank Duff

Giving away our faith.

Because she believes in God's universal plan of salvation, the Church must be missionary. (*CCC* 851)

Prayer for Today:

It is not enough to discover Christ—you must bring him to others! The world today is one great mission land, even in countries of longstanding Christian tradition.

Pope John Paul II

God our Father, to whom every human life is precious, you desire everyone "to be saved and to come to the knowledge of the truth" (1 Timothy 2:4).

But how can people believe in your Son if they don't hear of him—or don't hear enough? Send workers into your great harvest to preach your Gospel to every creature.

Send us!

Awaken our sense of mission.

Give us a sense of urgency so that we will bring Jesus to others as if it were a life-and-death matter.

Teach us how to win people to you by making them aware of your love.

Keep us faithful to your words.

Bishops, with priests as co-workers, have as their first task "to preach the Gospel of God to all men," in keeping with the Lord's command (cf Mk 16:15).

(CCC 888)[13]

Prayer for Today: Lord Jesus, when you preached on earth, you spoke with utter fidelity to the Father's will, saying nothing but what he had given you to say. And just before you returned to the Father by laying down your life on the cross, you entrusted that message to your apostles. "The words that you gave to me I have given to them," you told your Father (see John 17:8 NRSV).

We pray today for our pope and our bishops—successors of the Twelve—and for all who help them in their teaching mission, that they might transmit your word with absolute fidelity. May they proclaim your message with power and courage, with love and with the wisdom not of this world.

May we who hear your servants recognize in their words the voice and teaching of the faithful Shepherd—you who are the way, the truth, and the life.

The everyday offerings of a holy priesthood.

" ... worshipping everywhere by their holy actions, the laity consecrate the world itself to God, everywhere offering worship by the holiness of their lives" (cf. 1 Pet 2:5).

(CCC 901)[14]

Prayer for Today: Dear God, you call us to be salt, light, and leaven in those places where we spend our days—in cars, checkout lines, schools, factories, kitchens, hospitals, office cubicles.... How shall we bring your love into our daily haunts? How can we consecrate our little corners of the universe to you?

This is the essence of your vocation: to connect an ordinary and seemingly boring life with its repetitious details with Love who is God. Then boredom vanishes.... You must see the connection between this awareness, thoughtfulness, recollection, and the implementation and restoration of the world to Christ....

Christ is waiting for you to become aware of him and the work he has given you, by becoming aware of the connection between brooms, dishwater, letter typing ... and the restoration of the world.

Catherine Doherty

Strengthen your servants, Lord.

From the very beginning of the Church there were men and women who set out to follow Christ with greater liberty, and to imitate him more closely, by practicing the evangelical counsels.   (*CCC* 918)

Prayer for Today: Father, we thank you for giving your Church the witness of monks, hermits, members of religious orders, and all men and women living a consecrated life.

Strengthen your servants, who have left everything to follow you.

You have given them the desire to relinquish legitimate goods—the right to marriage, to possessions, to areas of decision-making—in order to give you more single-minded love and service.

Strengthen your servants, who have left everything to follow you.

May these men and women join themselves more and more closely to your Son, their hidden Spouse, so that they may be radiant pointers to the reality of the world to come, living images of the destiny of your whole people, whom you are preparing to be Christ's Bride.

Strengthen your servants, who have left everything to follow you.

Communion of saints, communion of goods.

"Since all the faithful form one body, the good of each is communicated to the others.... We must therefore believe that there exists a communion of goods in the Church."   (*CCC* 947)[15]

Reflection for Today: St. Thérèse of Lisieux made this reflection after watching a nun light many candles with a flame coaxed from a half-extinguished votive lamp:

It is the same with the communion of saints. Very often, without our knowing it, a hidden soul is responsible for the graces and lights we receive, because God wills that the saints communicate graces to each other through prayer.... How many times I've thought that perhaps I owe all the graces I've received to the prayers of a soul who asked God for them on my behalf and whom I will know only in heaven.

Christ offers me great spiritual riches through the intercession of the saints. Do I often ask for them?

Christ calls me to give generous spiritual assistance to other members of his Body—the dead who are being purified and the brothers and sisters who are my fellow pilgrims on earth. Do I pray for their needs?

The children of Eve implore the new Eve.

"We believe that the Holy Mother of God, the new Eve, Mother of the Church, continues in heaven to exercise her maternal role on behalf of the members of Christ." *Paul VI (CCC 975)*[16]

Prayer for Today: Pray the "Hail, Holy Queen" slowly, adding your own words to each phrase of the prayer, as the Spirit leads you. (If you like, use the italicized expansions to get you started.)

Hail, holy Queen,
Holy Mary, hailed by Gabriel as "full of grace" and crowned by Jesus as queen of heaven,
Mother of mercy,
Mother of Jesus, God's merciful love made flesh,
Hail, our life, our sweetness, and our hope.
How lovely and beautiful you are, Mary. Each thought of you is sweet to me.
To you do we cry, poor banished children of Eve.
To you do we send up our sighs,
mourning and weeping in this valley of tears.
Turn then, most gracious advocate,
your eyes of mercy on us,
and show us the blessed fruit of your womb, Jesus.
O clement, O loving, O sweet Virgin Mary.
Pray for us, O holy Mother of God,
that we may be worthy of the promises of Christ.

Jesus, you will raise us up at the last day.

"The confidence of Christians is the resurrection of the dead; believing this we live."

Tertullian (*CCC* 991)[17]

Prayer for Today: Lord Jesus, when Martha came to you grieving the death of her brother Lazarus (see John 11:20-27), you told her: "I am the resurrection and the life; he who believes in me, though he die, yet shall he live, and whoever lives and believes in me shall never die."

And then you asked Martha, "Do you believe this?"

Today, I want to make Martha's answer my own: "Yes, Lord; I believe." And even if I don't see in my earthly life what Martha saw in hers—a human corpse brought back to life at your command—I believe that I will see it on the last day.

Lord Jesus, you will raise up all those who have believed in you and have partaken of your body and blood! (see John 6:40, 54)

Jesus, your power will change our lowly bodies to be like your glorious body! (see Philippians 3:20-21)

Spirit of God, who raised Jesus from the dead, you will give new life to our mortal bodies! (See Romans 8:11.)

Remember the last things.

The Church encourages us to prepare ourselves for the hour of our death. (*CCC* 1014)

Prayer for Today: Ask St. Joseph, patron of the dying, to assist all those who are dying right now and to help you when your time comes. Pray a Hail Mary, with special attention to: "pray for us sinners, now and at the hour of our death."

Very soon your life here will end. Consider, then, what may be in store for you elsewhere. Today we live, tomorrow we die and are quickly forgotten. Oh, the dullness and hardness of a heart which looks only to the present instead of preparing for what is to come!

Therefore, in every deed and thought, act as though you were to die this very day. If you had a good conscience, you would not fear death very much. It is better to avoid sin than to fear death. If you are not prepared today, how will you be prepared tomorrow?

Thomas à Kempis

Sustained by the hope of heaven.

Heaven is the ultimate end and fulfillment of the deepest human longings, the state of supreme, definitive happiness.   (*CCC* 1024)

Reflection for Today: What is heaven like? While no one can really know, it can be instructive to meditate on the subject. Archbishop Fulton Sheen once suggested that we do this by thinking about the main joys we have known on earth: great moments when we felt a keen zest for life, discovered an exciting truth, or had an experience of love that we wanted to go on forever:

> Now suppose you could take this moment of life, raise it up to a focal point where it became the far deepest truth, raise it to infinity until it became the moment of the ecstasy of truth, and take that moment of love and eternalize it so that it became the Holy Spirit. Well, that gives some dim suggestion of what heaven is. It is perfect life ... perfect truth ... perfect love.

How unimaginably great is the reward you have prepared for those who love you, Lord! Help me to keep my eyes on the hope of heaven—especially when I'm feeling discouraged.

Let perpetual light shine upon them.

"Let us not hesitate to help those who have died and to offer our prayers for them."

St. John Chrysostom (*CCC* 1032)[18]

Prayer for Today: Father of mercies and God of all consolation, hear my prayer for all those who have died—especially for those I bring before you now. (*Take a few moments to think of the people you especially want to pray for.*)

Have mercy on those you called your sons and daughters on earth. Come to their aid, as they await the day when they will see you face to face. Bring the time of their purification to an end so that they may know the joy of being with you.

Welcome these departed brothers and sisters into the fullness of life, into the company of angels and saints who stand before your throne and offer unceasing praise. Through the merits of your Son, grant that we may we join them there one day.

Eternal rest grant unto them, O Lord, and let perpetual light shine upon them.

Today is the day of salvation.

The message of the Last Judgment calls men to conversion while God is still giving them "the acceptable time, ... the day of salvation" (2 Cor 6:2).

(*CCC* 1041)

Prayer for Today:
O come, let us sing to the Lord,
let us make a joyful noise to the rock of our salvation!
If today you hear his voice, harden not your hearts.

Let us come into his presence with thanksgiving,
let us offer him joyful songs of praise!
If today you hear his voice, harden not your hearts.

O come, let us worship and bow down,
let us kneel before the Lord, our Maker.
If today you hear his voice, harden not your hearts.

For he is our God, and we are the sheep of his pasture.
Let us be attentive and obedient to him.
If today you hear his voice, harden not your hearts.

adapted from Psalm 95

With eager longing for the new heavens and the new earth.

At the end of time, the Kingdom of God will come in its fullness. Then the just will reign with Christ for ever, glorified in body and soul, and the material universe itself will be transformed. (*CCC* 1060)

Prayer for Today:
Praise to you, O God!
In the beginning you created the heavens and the earth.
At the end, you will create a new heaven and a new earth.

Together with your whole creation, we long for this full coming of your Kingdom.
We yearn for the day when we will dwell with you in the heavenly Jerusalem,
where death and tears will be no more.
You will be our light, and we will share in your glory.
We will be your spotless Bride.

May your Kingdom come, Lord.
May it come in us. May we hasten its coming into the world around us.

"The Spirit and the Bride say, 'Come.' And let him who hears say, 'Come.' And let him who is thirsty come, let him who desires take the water of life without price" (Revelation 22:17).

We come, Lord.
And with joyful hope we say, "Come, Lord Jesus!"

PART TWO
Lord, We Remember

Part two of the *Catechism*, "The Celebration of the Christian Mystery," focuses on liturgical prayer, especially the seven sacraments. Liturgy being essentially corporate—a visible, public action of the Church which involves the participation of all its members—you might wonder how it relates to personal prayer. The *Catechism* makes this connection quite clear:

> In the sacramental liturgy of the Church, the mission of Christ and of the Holy Spirit proclaims, makes present, and communicates the mystery of salvation, which is continued in the heart that prays. The spiritual writers sometimes compare the heart to an altar. Prayer internalizes and assimilates the liturgy during and after its celebration. (*CCC* 2655)

The better we understand the liturgy, the more we meditate on its words and signs and symbols, the more it will transform and unify every aspect of our life. Praying this part of the *Catechism* is a way to grow in this understanding and to develop a "heart that prays."

Then, enriched by our personal prayer, we will approach the sacraments with greater joy—eager to participate through them in Christ's prayer to the Father through the Holy Spirit, eager to remember and celebrate the Paschal mystery by which we have been saved.

Celebrate the history of our salvation!

"The wonderful works of God among the people of the Old Testament were but a prelude to the work of Christ the Lord in redeeming mankind and giving perfect glory to God." (*CCC* 1067)[19]

Prayer for Today:
Jesus, as the Word, you brought all creation into being.
Give thanks to the Lord, for his love is everlasting.

You are the new Moses, leading your people out of slavery and into the Kingdom.
Give thanks to the Lord, for his love is everlasting.

The prophets foretold the coming Messiah, the King of kings.
Give thanks to the Lord, for his love is everlasting.

Born in a lowly manger, you lived among us as a carpenter's son.
Give thanks to the Lord, for his love is everlasting.

Through your obedience, death was vanquished and we are reborn.
Give thanks to the Lord, for his love is everlasting.

Now you are seated at the Father's right hand in glory.
Give thanks to the Lord, for his love is everlasting.

Entering into heaven's worship.

"In the earthly liturgy we share in a foretaste of that heavenly liturgy which is celebrated in the Holy City of Jerusalem toward which we journey as pilgrims, where Christ is sitting at the right hand of God...."

(*CCC* 1090)[20]

Prayer for Today: The book of Revelation offers a rich picture of the heavenly liturgy that resounds in the Church's official worship, especially the Eucharist. Reflect on the following verses and make their prayers your own today. (If you can, read Revelation 4:6-11 and 5:1-14).

"Holy, holy, holy, is the Lord God Almighty, who was and is and is to come!" (4:8b).

"Worthy is the Lamb who was slain, to receive power and wealth and wisdom and might and honor and glory and blessing!" (5:12).

And the four living creatures said, "Amen!" (5:14).

Jesus, you are the link between the liturgy of earth and the liturgy of heaven.... United to [your] praises, the prayer of the Church, becomes divine and the liturgy of the earth becomes one with that of the celestial hierarchies in the court of Christ.

Jean-Baptist Chautard

The Holy Spirit is artisan of the liturgy.

In the liturgy the Holy Spirit is teacher of the faith of the People of God and artisan of "God's master-pieces," the sacraments of the New Covenant.

(*CCC* 1091)

Prayer for Today:
Holy Spirit, teacher of prayer,
you lead us to pray in thanksgiving for the Father's count-less blessings;
you help us to respond with our own blessings of thanks and praise.

Spirit of the promise,
you prepare us to meet Jesus in the liturgy,
awakening faith, preparing hearts to be fertile soil where good seed can take root.

Spirit of truth,
you make God's word come alive for us,
unfolding its meaning and significance
so that it becomes an encounter with the living Word, Jesus, in whom we see the Father.

Breath of life,
you breathe life into every liturgical celebration
so that it becomes what it represents,
and we are made participants, not spectators, in the sav-ing mysteries.

continued on next page

Spirit of Christ,
you gather God's scattered children together into the one
Body of Christ;
you live in us as a burning flame of love
to help us offer our lives as a living sacrifice and bear lasting fruit in your service.

Jesus' power still comes forth.

Sacraments are "powers that come forth" from the Body of Christ (cf. Lk 5:17; 6:19; 8:46), which is ever-living and life-giving. They are actions of the Holy Spirit at work in his Body, the Church. (*CCC* 1116)

Prayer for Today: Lord Jesus, while you were on earth, you were surrounded by so many people who needed your works of power. Like that ailing woman in the crowd—the one who reached out in faith to touch the hem of your cloak (see Luke 8:43-48).

How astonished she must have been to be healed! And then to be singled out by you: "Who was it that touched me?... Some one touched me; for I perceive that power has gone forth from me."

Lord Jesus, I'm just as needy as that woman. Maybe more so. And so I'm grateful that you are just as present to me as you were to her. Through the sacraments, divine power still comes forth from you. I touch you in faith, and you make me whole.

The sacraments bring God near.

A sacramental celebration is woven from signs and symbols. (*CCC* 1145)

Prayer for Today: Blessed are you, Holy Trinity, for not leaving us to make our way to you unaided and unaccompanied. Blessed are you for giving us the sacraments, with their visible signs and symbols that speak to our senses and make invisible realities present to us.

Who but you, O God, could have conceived of such a marvelous plan? Bread, water, words, even simple gestures—the stuff of daily life—are blessed and fashioned to give us special access to you. Ordinary signs and symbols are given extraordinary ability to bring about the saving graces that they signify.

We bless you for the sacraments!

A sacrament is not only a commemorative sign of something which is now past—the passion of Christ. It is also a demonstrative sign of something now present and caused in us by the passion of Christ—grace. Further, it is a ... prophetic sign of something as yet in the future—glory.

St. Thomas Aquinas

Just looking, Lord.

Christian iconography expresses in images the same Gospel message that Scripture communicates by words. Image and word illuminate each other.

(*CCC* 1160)

Reflection for Today: Have you ever tried turning to God simply by gazing at a crucifix, statue, or picture of a Gospel scene? St. Teresa of Avila, one of many spiritual writers who recommend this prayerful gazing, never tired of contemplating her picture of the Samaritan woman at the well (see John 4:7-26). Christians in the Eastern tradition contemplate icons, sacred images intended to serve as windows onto eternal realities.

There are many times when I cannot pray, when I am too tired to read the gospels, too restless to have spiritual thoughts, too depressed to find words for God, or too exhausted to do anything. But I can still look at these images [icons] so intimately connected with the experience of love.

Henri Nouwen

Today, spend five or ten minutes contemplating an icon or other representation of a Christian reality. Let the Holy Spirit use this visible aid to draw you into the invisible mysteries, into the heart of God.

Illumined by the Feast of feasts.

The mystery of the Resurrection, in which Christ crushed death, permeates with its powerful energy our old time, until all is subjected to him.   (*CCC* 1169)

Prayer for Today:
Christ is risen!
He is risen indeed!

The light of his Resurrection fills the whole world
   and floods each day with its brilliance.
His victory is the Feast, giving radiance
   to every other feast and season:
- to Sunday—the Lord's day, the day of Christians who look in hope to the glory of the new Jerusalem,
- to Advent, with its patient longing for the Light,
- to the Christmas season, when the Word leaped down from heaven to scatter the night darkness,
- to Lenten disciplines, preparing the way for the King of glory,
- to the feasts of Mary and the saints,

who conquered death by the blood of the Lamb
and who shine like stars as they reign with Christ.
A new age has dawned!
The light of Christ has come into the world,
has come into *today*.

Christ is risen!
He is risen indeed!

Make us your temple, O God.

... visible churches are not simply gathering places but signify and make visible the Church living in this place, the dwelling of God with men reconciled and united in Christ. (*CCC* 1180)

Prayer for Today: Jesus, you whose body is the new temple where God's glory dwells, we thank you for your presence in our churches. Thank you for recognizing the house of your Father in these houses of prayer. Thank you for coming to dwell in them as you dwell in the Church, which you are building, stone by living stone. As we gather to pray and to worship you in our churches, make us living temples of your Holy Spirit.

Lord, you know how weak and distracted we are and how we consider everything else more important than you; but again and again you guide us back to this place where you dwell in order to change us.

Adrienne von Speyr

We adore you, Christ, here and in all your churches in the whole world, and we bless you because by your holy cross you have redeemed the world.

St. Francis of Assisi

Thanks for life-giving waters.

"In Baptism we use your gift of water, which you have made a rich symbol of the grace you give us in this sacrament." (*CCC* 1217)[21]

Reflection for Today: What makes water such a rich symbol for the grace we receive in Baptism? Take a few minutes to reflect prayerfully on the connection between water and Baptism in some of the events of salvation history. You might think about one or two of the following:

- creation, with God's Spirit "moving over the face of the waters" (Genesis 1:2)
- the great flood and Noah's ark (see Genesis 6-8)
- the parting of the Red Sea and Israel's release from slavery (see Exodus 14)
- Jesus' own baptism and anointing by the Spirit (see Mark 1:9-11)
- Jesus pierced by a spear as he hung on the cross (see John 19:34)

Father, thank you for your gift of water. Thank you for the waters of Baptism, which bury us into Christ's death and plunge us into your own life. And thank you, too, for holy water, which reminds us of our new life in you.

I renew my promises to you, my God.

He [the baptismal candidate] explicitly renounces Satan. Thus prepared, he is able to *confess the faith of the Church,* to which he will be "entrusted" by Baptism (cf. Rom 6:17). (*CCC* 1237)

Prayer for Today: "Take the whole armor of God, that you may be able to withstand in the evil day.... Stand therefore, having girded your loins with truth, ... taking the shield of faith, with which you can quench all the flaming darts of the evil one" (Ephesians 6:13-14, 16).

Dear God,
I want to walk as your child.
I reject Satan and all his works and empty promises.
I reject sin. I want to live in your freedom.
I reject sin's power. I will fight so as not to let it master me.

I believe in you, O God, Father, Son, and Holy Spirit.
I believe all the truths you have given me through your Church.

Help me to put on your armor and stand firm today and every day.
Bring me to life everlasting with you.

Amen.

We belong to Christ.

Christians are also marked with a seal.... This seal of the Holy Spirit marks our total belonging to Christ, our enrollment in his service for ever.... (*CCC* 1296)[22]

Prayer for Today: As the Father put his seal on you, Lord Jesus, so you have put your seal on me (see John 6:27; 2 Corinthians 1:22). What a privilege it is to be yours! Today, help me to remember that I am not my own and to live accordingly. Teach me to surrender myself whole-heartedly to you, as you surrendered yourself to the Father's will.

Take, Lord, all my liberty. Receive my memory, my understanding, and my whole will. Whatever I have and possess, you have given me; to you I restore it wholly, and to your will I utterly surrender it for my direction. Give me only your love, with your grace, and I am rich enough; nor do I ask anything besides.

St. Ignatius Loyola

Pentecost goes on!

... the effect of the sacrament of Confirmation is the special outpouring of the Holy Spirit as once granted to the apostles on the day of Pentecost.

(*CCC* 1302)

Reflection for Today:
How can we not give thanks to God for the wonders the Spirit has never ceased to accomplish in these two millenniums of Christian life? Indeed, the event of grace at Pentecost has continued to bear its marvelous fruits, everywhere instilling apostolic zeal, a desire for contemplation, the commitment to live and serve God and our brothers and sisters with complete dedication. Today too, the Spirit sustains great and small acts of forgiveness and prophecy in the Church and gives life to ever new charisms and gifts, which attest to his ceaseless action in human hearts.

Pope John Paul II

Holy Spirit, have your way with us! Let your fire fall afresh on us to burn out every evil from our hearts and fill us with zeal for your work. Loosen our tongues to proclaim your truth. Lead us in new ways. Make us more like Christ in bearing witness to the world.

Devoutly I adore you.

The Eucharist is the heart and the summit of the Church's life, for in it Christ associates his Church and all her members with his sacrifice of praise and thanksgiving…. by this sacrifice he pours out the graces of salvation on his Body which is the Church. (*CCC* 1407)

Prayer for Today:
Eternal and all-powerful God,
I approach the sacrament of your only Son, our Lord Jesus Christ.
I come as a sick person to the Physician of life,
as one who needs bathing to the fountain of mercy,
as a blind person to the light of eternal splendor;
poor and needy, I come to the Lord of heaven and earth.

O most gracious God,
may I receive the Body of your only-begotten Son,
our Lord Jesus Christ, born of the Virgin Mary,
so that I might be worthy to be joined to his mystical Body
and counted among his members.
Most loving Father,
give me your beloved Son,
whom I now prepare to receive in this hidden form,
but hope to contemplate face to face for all eternity.

from a prayer before communion
by St. Thomas Aquinas

To whom else shall we go, Lord?

"Will you also go away?" (Jn 6:67): the Lord's question echoes through the ages, as a loving invitation to discover that only he has "the words of eternal life" (Jn 6:68) and that to receive in faith the gift of his Eucharist is to receive the Lord himself.   (*CCC* 1336)

Reflection for Today:

Yes, in bread Christ has become so simple—has condescended so far that a child can eat the Sacred Food with love and gratitude. He said that we would be scandalized.... Even the nearest and dearest of his friends dispersed and fled, not realizing the mystery of the Redemption....

It took me a long time as a convert to realize the presence of Christ as Man in the sacrament. He is the same Jesus who walked on earth, who slept in the boat as the tempest arose, who hungered in the desert, who prayed in the garden, who conversed with the woman by the well, who rested at the house of Martha and Mary, who wandered through the cornfields, picking the ears of corn to eat.

Jesus is there as Man. He is there, Flesh and Blood, Soul and Divinity. He is our leader who is always with us.

Dorothy Day

The Food of heaven nourishes and changes us.

By giving himself to us Christ revives our love and enables us to break our disordered attachments to creatures and root ourselves in him.   (*CCC* 1394)

Prayer for Today: Jesus, you said that whoever eats your flesh and drinks your blood would live in you, and you in them (see John 6:56). Lord, as we receive you in the Eucharist, come and live in us. O you who are love, unite us to yourself and to one another. Break our bonds of sin, and strengthen the bonds of charity among us.

Your great intention in receiving communion should be to advance, strengthen, and comfort yourself in the love of God.... If worldly people ask why you receive Communion so often, tell them that it is to learn to love God, be purified from your imperfections, delivered from misery, comforted in affliction, and supported in weakness.

St. Francis de Sales

Repent and believe the Good News.

Christ's call to conversion continues to resound in the lives of Christians. This *second conversion* is an uninterrupted task for the whole Church.... (*CCC* 1428)

Prayer for Today: Merciful Savior, thank you for making me a child of God. And thank you for not giving up on me when I turn away from you. Today, Lord, increase my love for you so that I may hear and act on your call to continuing conversion.

"Repent, for the kingdom of heaven is at hand" (Matthew 4:17).
"Believe in God, believe also in me" (John 14:1).
"Go, and do not sin again" (John 8:11)

I hear you, Lord!

Conversion ought to be going on every day, since self-centeredness is ever-living. They say it dies a few hours after we ourselves are dead.

Dom Helder Camara

Forgive me, for I have sinned.

"Whoever confesses his sins ... is already working with God. God indicts your sins; if you also indict them, you are joined with God.... The beginning of good works is the confession of evil works."

St. Augustine (*CCC* 1458)[23]

Prayer for Today:
Have mercy on me, O God,
according to your steadfast love;
according to your abundant mercy
blot out my transgressions.
Wash me thoroughly from my iniquity,
and cleanse me from my sin!

For I know my transgressions,
and my sin is ever before me.
Against you, you alone, have I sinned,
and done that which is evil in your sight.

Create in me a clean heart, O God,
and put a new and right spirit within me.
Cast me not away from your presence,
and take not your holy Spirit from me.
Restore to me the joy of your salvation,
and uphold me with a willing spirit.

Then I will teach transgressors your ways,
and sinners will return to you.
O Lord, open my lips,
and my mouth will declare your praise.

adapted from Psalm 51

We suffer in union with Christ.

By his passion and death on the cross Christ has given a new meaning to suffering: it can henceforth configure us to him and unite us with his redemptive Passion. (*CCC* 1505)

Prayer for Today: Lord Jesus, you suffered and died for love of me. May I endure my sufferings for love of you. In all my trials, may I be sustained by remembering what you did for me—in the garden of Gethsemane, before the chief priests and Pilate, on the bloody road to Golgotha, on the cross. Teach me how to unite my suffering to yours so that it may bear fruit for your Kingdom and make me more like you.

Our participation in the paschal mystery—in the suffering, death, and resurrection of Jesus—brings a certain *freedom:* the freedom to let go, to surrender ourselves to the living God, to place ourselves completely in his hands.... It's precisely in letting go, in entering into complete union with the Lord, in letting him take over, that we discover our true selves.

Cardinal Joseph Bernardin

The Lord will raise them up.

"Through this holy anointing may the Lord in his love and mercy help you with the grace of the Holy Spirit. May the Lord who frees you from sin save you and raise you up." (*CCC* 1513)[24]

Prayer for Today:
O God, source of all life and health,
we ask your special blessing on all our brothers and sisters
who struggle with suffering, illness, and disease.

We bring before you those who will receive
the Anointing of the Sick today.
We remember those undergoing surgery
or other medical treatments,
all those in hospitals, nursing homes,
psychiatric care units....
We pray for those whose ailments are less serious,
but still painful and troubling,
for the elderly, as they face the challenges of aging,
and for all caregivers and medical personnel.

Lord Jesus, you bore our suffering and carried our griefs.
Show your healing power to all who need it.

Is any among you sick? Let him call for the elders of the church, and let them pray over him, anointing him with oil in the name of the Lord; and the prayer of faith will save the sick man, and the Lord will raise him up; and if he has committed sins, he will be forgiven.

JAMES 5:14-15

Making Christ's presence visible.

In the ecclesial service of the ordained minister, it is Christ himself who is present to his Church as Head of his Body, Shepherd of his flock, high priest of the redemptive sacrifice, Teacher of Truth. (*CCC* 1548)

Reflection for Today: Do I ever think about the fact that Jesus is present to me in a special way in the person of the priest? At Mass, does it ever strike me that it is Christ himself offering the Eucharistic sacrifice through the ministry of the priest? Would I approach the sacrament of Reconciliation more eagerly or more often if I thought of the priest in the confessional as both the sign and the instrument of God's saving love for me?

Approach a priest with the understanding that he has God in him in a special manner through his ordination. Approach him as you would approach Christ.

Catherine Doherty

The priest continues the work of redemption on earth…. The Priesthood is the love of the heart of Jesus.

St. John Vianney (CCC 1589)[25]

Holy Orders: call to become "another Christ."

The grace of the Holy Spirit proper to this sacrament is configuration to Christ as Priest, Teacher, and Pastor, of whom the ordained is made a minister.

(CCC 1585)

Prayer for Today:

.... O Mother of the Church,
in the midst of the disciples in the upper room
you prayed to the Spirit
for the new people and their shepherds;
obtain for the Order of Presbyters
a full measure of gifts,
O Queen of the Apostles.

O Mother of Jesus Christ,
you were with him at the beginning
of his life and mission;
you sought the Master among the crowd;
you stood beside him
when he was lifted up from the earth,
consumed as the one eternal sacrifice;
and you had John, your son, near at hand;
accept from the beginning those
who have been called;
protect their growth,
in their life ministry, accompany your sons,
O Mother of Priests. Amen.

from a prayer by Pope John Paul II

Two for holiness.

"God himself is the author of marriage."

(*CCC* 1603)[26]

Prayer for Today: Lord, your word says, "it is not good that the man should be alone" (Genesis 2:18). Marriage was *your* idea. Out of love you created man and woman for each another and called them to mutual love in you.

Bless all married couples with fruitful, faithful love.

There was a marriage at Cana in Galilee, and the mother of Jesus was there; Jesus also was invited to the marriage, with his disciples.

JOHN 2:1-2

Jesus, by attending the wedding feast and working your first sign there, you confirmed the goodness of marriage and made it a sign of your presence.

Make your presence known in the lives of those you have joined together.

For this reason a man shall leave his father and mother and be joined to his wife, and the two shall become one flesh. This mystery is a profound one, and I am saying that it refers to Christ and the church.

EPHESIANS 5:31-32

Father, you made the union of husband and wife a holy mystery and a symbol of the deepest love.

Let it call us all to seek intimacy with you.

For the children in my life.

"Children are the supreme gift of marriage and con-
tribute greatly to the good of the parents themselves."
(*CCC* 1652)[27]

Reflection for Today: Make this a special day of prayer
for your children—or for grandchildren, godchildren,
nieces and nephews, or other children you know. Bring
each one quietly before the Lord. Think about their
uniqueness, their needs, their own special call to holiness.
Decide how you will remember to pray for them later
today. Then bring them before the Lord in your own
words, or use the following prayer as a starter.

Father, see all these children present in my heart as I come
before you. Each one is such a gift from you.

Jesus, I picture you taking each one into your arms,
putting your hands on their heads as a sign of your blessing.

Holy Spirit, watch over these young lives.
Give your wisdom to everyone entrusted with their care
and protection.

God, give us your love for these children
and a deep desire to see your plan for them fulfilled.
Make up for our oversights, failures, and inadequacies.
Give us hearts of love.

At home in Nazareth.

Christ chose to be born and grow up in the bosom of the holy family of Joseph and Mary. (*CCC* 1655)

Prayer for Today: You might have done things differently, Lord. You might have come among us in a more visibly powerful way, with hosts of angels surrounding you. But who of us would have dared to approach you then?

Thank you for veiling your glory and for choosing to be born into a real family. Thank you for living our life. Thank you that the door to your home in Nazareth remains open, and that we can slip inside and learn from you and Mary and Joseph how to live our everyday lives in a way that glorifies the Father.

A real mother, a real father, and a real Child, living, loving, suffering—not symbols, but people like us.... That means ... we must treat the Holy Family in a way as our next-door neighbors, become acquainted with them, invite them over, watch them all the while, and ponder about them in our hearts.

Maria von Trapp

The Glorious cross of Jesus.

... the Church imparts blessings by invoking the name of Jesus, usually while making the holy sign of the cross of Christ. (*CCC* 1671)

Reflection for Today: This twelfth-century reflection on the cross offers rich possibilities for meditation:

We venerate the cross as a safeguard of faith, as the strengthening of hope, and the throne of love. It is the sign of mercy, the proof of forgiveness, the vehicle of grace and the banner of peace....

The cross of Christ is the door to heaven, the key to paradise, the downfall of the devil, the uplifting of mankind, the consolation of our imprisonment, the prize for our freedom.... Tyrants are convicted by the cross and the mighty ones defeated; it lifts up the miserable and honors the poor. The cross is the end of darkness, the spreading of light, the flight of death, the ship of life, and the kingdom of salvation....

By the cross Christ draws everything to him. It is the kingdom of the Father, the scepter of the Son, and the seal of the Holy Spirit, a witness to the total Trinity.

St. Rupert of Deutz

Be with me in my final journey.

The Christian who dies in Christ Jesus is "away from the body and at home with the Lord" (2 Cor 5:8).

(*CCC* 1681)

Prayer for Today:
Because you endured and conquered death
    for love of me, Lord Jesus,
I can willingly accept the death
    through which you will bring me home to be with you.
I am full of fears and anxieties,
    but I take heart when I remember your words:

"I am the resurrection and the life ... whoever lives and believes in me will never die" (John 11:25-26).

"Today you will be with me in paradise" (Luke 23:43b).

And so I accept from your merciful hands whatever is to come.
I commit my dying to you.
Sustain me in my final hours
    by the powerful weapons of your sacraments,
    by the prayers of your Mother,
    your earthly father, Saint Joseph,
    and all my patron saints.

Grant that I may die in your faith, in your service, in your love, with holy mother Church accompanying me at journey's end to surrender me into the Father's hands. Amen.

PART THREE
Lord, We Follow

"Life in Christ," part three of the *Catechism*, is a sort of reality check. This is the section that tells us how Christ's followers are to conduct themselves and that sets out the objective standards by which we can assess our faithfulness. Namely, we are to live in the light of the Beatitudes (see Matthew 5:3-12) and in obedience to the law of charity toward God and neighbor, as specified in the Ten Commandments (see Exodus 20:1-17; Deuteronomy 5:6-22).

As you meditate on this part of the *Catechism*, you might find it helpful to ponder these scripture passages, as well as Jesus' summary of the commandments: "You shall love the Lord your God with all your heart, and with all your soul, and with all your mind, and with all your strength.... You shall love your neighbor as yourself" (Mark 12:30, 31).

With its emphasis on what it takes to live as Christ's disciple—the struggle to reject sin and cultivate virtue—this section of the *Catechism* lends itself naturally to prayer centered on examining our conscience and asking for God's mercy. But prayers of praise and thanksgiving are in order, too, as we consider our vocation to eternal happiness and the grace and spiritual gifts that God gives us to attain it.

Blessed are the desperate.

The Beatitudes ... shed light on the actions and attitudes characteristic of the Christian life; they are the paradoxical promises that sustain hope in the midst of tribulations....   (*CCC* 1717)

Prayer for Today:

Blessed are the poor in spirit,
for theirs is the kingdom of heaven.
Blessed are those who mourn,
for they shall be comforted.
Blessed are the meek,
for they shall inherit the earth....
Blessed are the merciful,
for they shall obtain mercy....
Blessed are those who are persecuted for righteousness' sake,
for theirs is the kingdom of heaven.

MATTHEW 5:3-5, 7, 10

Jesus, what a strange way of life you sketch out for me in the Beatitudes.

Blessed are the desperate, they tell me. Blessed are those who seek their happiness in things unseen.

Help me to take these paradoxical sayings more seriously, to seek you above all else, to live as if I really believed that in your kingdom, the first shall be last.

continued on next page

Most of these things had been spoken of, and right endurance of them praised, in the Old Testament. But they had hardly been described as adding up to blessedness…. Mercy and cleanness of heart, yes. But sorrow, persecution, reviling, and slander? Jesus is wholly uncompromising about these things.

Frank Sheed

For freedom Christ has set us free.

The more one does what is good, the freer one becomes. There is no true freedom except in the service of what is good and just.   (*CCC* 1733)

Prayer for Today:
Lord Jesus, shall we delay our sacrifice to you of all we have, our offering to you of all we are? Shall we keep back any longer the complete gift of our free will, the one power of our souls that means so much to us? Shall we refuse to stretch it out on the wood of your cross...? If only free will would die to self, to burn continuously for you!

Free will enjoys its greatest freedom when devoted to God's service; never more enslaved but when entirely at our command. It is never more alive as when it dies to self; never so dead if it lives for self alone. We are free to do good or evil; but we are abusing—instead of using—our freedom, when we choose evil.

St. Francis de Sales

The key to honest self-evaluation.

Human acts, that is, acts that are freely chosen in consequence of a judgment of conscience, can be morally evaluated. They are either good or evil. (*CCC* 1749)

Prayer for Today:
Dear Father, searcher of hearts, you know us through and through.

You know our distaste for truthful self-assessment.

You see how reluctant we are to own our actions and take responsibility for them. We justify ourselves by blaming others—and even you!—for our sins and failures. When we do good, we quickly take the credit.

Loving Father, help us to evaluate our lives honestly, without shrinking from pronouncing our actions good or evil, according to your standards.

When we do good, teach us to praise you for it, with thanks for the grace that made it possible.

When we sin, teach us to return to you quickly, with confidence in your abiding love.

"Come now, let us reason together," you gently encourage us (Isaiah 1:18).

Father, we come!

Your law is my delight.

In the formation of conscience the Word of God is the light for our path (cf. Ps 119:105); we must assimilate it in faith and prayer and put it into practice.

(*CCC* 1785)

Prayer for Today:
O Lord, how I love your word!
I meditate on it all day long.
I lay it up in my heart,
that I might not sin against you.
I think about your precepts and fix my eyes on your ways.
I delight in your statutes.
I will not forget your word.

Teach me your way, Lord, and I will keep it to the end.
Give me understanding, that I may keep your law
and observe it with my whole heart.
Lead me along your path, for I delight in it.
Teach me good judgment and knowledge,
that I may reject every false way.
Enlarge my understanding,
and I will run in the way of your commandments!

O Lord,
your word is a lamp to my feet and a light to my path.
Open my eyes,
that I may always behold wondrous things in it!

inspired by Psalm 119

The evangelizing power of virtue.

The virtuous person tends toward the good with all his sensory and spiritual powers; he pursues the good and chooses it in concrete actions. (*CCC* 1803)

Reflection for Today: The mystic Hildegard of Bingen said that growing in virtue is like receiving a treasure from someone who loves you. If you love your benefactor too, she noted, you'll ponder how to get the maximum profit out of his gift—not primarily to enrich yourself but to increase both his public standing and his affection for you.

We should do the same in relation to God, said Hildegard, for he loves us greatly and offers us the best treasure of all, a keen intelligence:

Profit from your intellect in good works and grow rich in virtue, that he, the good Giver, may thereby be clearly known.... Think often about how to make so great a gift as useful to others as to yourself by works of justice, so that you will reflect the splendor of sanctity, and people will be inspired by your good example to praise and honor God.

Hildegard of Bingen

Prayer for the "hinge" virtues.

Four virtues play a pivotal role and accordingly are called "cardinal"; all the others are grouped around them. (*CCC* 1805)

Prayer for Today: I am a self-protective servant, Lord. "Be prudent," I tell myself when decisions must be made. "Protect yourself" is what I tend to mean. Train me in true *prudence*, so that I may always see the right way to achieve your purposes and embrace whatever risks are involved.

I am a selfish servant, Lord, more intent on securing my rights than on giving others their due. Train me in *justice*, that I may offer you a rightful sacrifice of praise and seek justice for my neighbor.

I am a cowardly servant, Lord. How halfheartedly I resist even small temptations! Train me in *fortitude:* I don't want to love my life so much that I would refuse to lose it for your sake.

I am immoderate, Lord, in the way I pursue pleasure. Train me in *temperance*, that I may enjoy your creation wisely and honorably.

I believe, Lord.

By faith, we believe in God and believe all that he has revealed to us and that Holy Church proposes for our belief. (*CCC* 1842)

Prayer for Today:
"The word is near you, on your lips and in your heart (that is, the word of faith which we preach)" (Romans 10:8). Believe, and you have found…. Seek, then, with confidence, seek with zeal. The Lord is good to the soul that seeks him (see Lamentations 3:25). Seek him by your prayers, seek him by your actions, find him by your faith. What is there that faith does not find? It attains the unreachable, it discovers the hidden, grasps the immeasurable, embraces the farthest depths; in a certain manner, it even contains eternity itself with its great expanse.

I say with confidence that I believe in the blessed and eternal Trinity, which I do not understand: I hold by faith that which I do not grasp with my mind.

St. Bernard of Clairvaux

This hope does not disappoint.

"Hope, O my soul, hope…. Dream that the more you struggle, the more you prove the love that you bear your God, and the more you will rejoice one day with your Beloved, in a happiness and rapture that can never end."   *St. Teresa of Avila* (*CCC* 1821)[28]

Prayer for Today: God of mercy, power, and truth, who has ever put their hope in you and been disappointed? Who has ever known you to deceive or break a promise? Sure of your faithfulness, I place all my trust in you, my God. You have given me the hope of heaven: may this hope stay fresh and alive in me, sustaining me through every hardship. Strengthen me to do your will joyfully, selflessly, for love of you and with my eyes on the prize of eternal life.

Hope is faith directed to the future…. Hope ultimately means that my implicit desire for God is God's own trace in my being. Hope means that my agony and ecstasy of longing for a joy this world can never give is a sure sign that I was made for him who is Joy, and him alone.

Peter Kreeft

Making love our aim.

"If I ... have not charity," says the Apostle, "I am nothing" (1 Cor 13:1-4).   (*CCC* 1826)

Reflection for Today: Read through a favorite scripture passage that focuses on love, such as 1 Corinthians 13; John 15:9-13; 1 John 4:7-21. Linger over any words or phrases that catch your attention. Or reflect on one or more of these verses:

"As the Father has loved me, so have I loved you; abide in my love" (John 15:9).

"This is my commandment, that you love one another as I have loved you" (John 15:12).

"But I say to you, Love your enemies and pray for those who persecute you" (Matthew 5:44).

Love bears all things, believes all things, hopes all things, endures all things (1 Corinthians 13:7).

If we love one another, God abides in us and his love is perfected in us (1 John 4:12).

My God, because you are so good, I love you with my whole heart—at least, I *want* to! And for your sake, I love my neighbor as myself—at least, I *want* to! Please help me remember to tell you this often today.

With your sevenfold gifts descend!

The seven *gifts* of the Holy Spirit ... complete and perfect the virtues of those who receive them. They make the faithful docile in readily obeying divine inspirations.
(*CCC* 1831)

Prayer for Today:

Holy Spirit, who proceed from the Father and the Son, *enter our hearts.*

Holy Spirit, who are equal to the Father and the Son, *enter our hearts.*

Promise of the Father, *have mercy on us.*
Ray of heavenly light, *have mercy on us.*
Source of heavenly water, *have mercy on us.*
Consuming Fire, *have mercy on us.*
Ardent Charity, *have mercy on us.*
Spiritual Anointing, *have mercy on us.*

Spirit of wisdom and understanding, *have mercy on us.*
Spirit of counsel and fortitude, *have mercy on us.*
Spirit of knowledge and piety, *have mercy on us.*
Spirit of the fear of the Lord, *have mercy on us.*

Holy Spirit, *shed your light into our souls.*
Holy Spirit, *engrave your law in our hearts.*
Holy Spirit, *enlighten us with your heavenly inspirations.*
Holy Spirit, *lead us in the way of salvation.*
Holy Spirit, *inspire us in the practice of good.*
Holy Spirit, *be our everlasting reward.*

adapted from a litany of the Holy Spirit

Jesus, you vanquished sin!

...at the very hour of darkness,... the sacrifice of Christ secretly becomes the source from which the forgiveness of our sins will pour forth inexhaustibly.

(*CCC* 1851)

Prayer for Today:
We adore you, O Christ, and we praise you.
Because by your holy cross, you have redeemed the world.

O my dying Jesus, I kiss devoutly the cross on which you died for love of me. Because of my sins, I deserved to die a miserable death; but your death is my hope. By the merits of your death, give me the grace to die embracing your feet and burning with love for you. I commit my soul into your hands. I love you with my whole heart. I repent of ever having sinned against you. Never let me sin against you again. Let me love you always, and then do with me as you will.

St. Alphonsus Liguori

Those insidious "little" sins.

But do not despise these sins which we call "light": if you take them for light when you weigh them, tremble when you count them.

St. Augustine (*CCC* 1863)[29]

Prayer for Today:
"It's no big deal."
"Everybody does it."
"I'm only human."
"I'm still a nice person."
"What's the harm in something so little?"

Forgive me, Lord, for my excuses and complacency.
Forgive me for underestimating the seriousness of every
    sin.
Forgive me for tolerating—and even befriending—some
    of the things you hate.
Forgive me for not standing guard against the "little"
    sins that chip away at our friendship.
Forgive me for not really believing
    that you want to make me perfect.
Forgive me for getting so discouraged at my failures
    that I forget your grace.
Forgive me for every time I've betrayed your love for
    me.
Forgive me, Lord.

continued on next page

Venial sin, no matter how small it is, displeases God....
But if venial sin displeases God, the desire and attach-
ment we have to venial sin is nothing else than a determination to want to displease him. Is it possible that a
generous person is not only determined to displease
God but is fond of displeasing him?

St. Francis de Sales

Return to God with all your heart.

Where sin has perverted the social climate, it is necessary to call for the conversion of hearts and appeal to the grace of God. Charity urges just reforms.

(*CCC* 1896)[30]

Prayer for Today:
"Thus says the Lord of hosts, Render true judgments, show kindness and mercy each to his brother, do not oppress the widow, the fatherless, the sojourner, or the poor; and let none of you devise evil against his brother in your heart."   ZECHARIAH 7:9-10
May we turn from sin and embrace the gospel.

"Is not this the fast that I choose: to loose the bonds of wickedness, to undo the thongs of the yoke, to let the oppressed go free, and to break every yoke? Is it not to share your bread with the hungry, and bring the homeless poor into your house; when you see the naked, to cover him?   ISAIAH 58:6-7
May we turn from sin and embrace the gospel.

"Return to me with all your heart, with fasting, with weeping, and with mourning; and rend your hearts and not your garments."   JOEL 2:12-13
May we turn from sin and embrace the gospel.

One loving Father of all.

The unity of the human family, embracing people who enjoy equal natural dignity, implies a *universal common good*. (*CCC* 1911)

Prayer for Today:
Father, you have given life to all the peoples of the earth. With great love, you called each man, woman, and child into being.

You know each of us by name: no one is insignificant to you. How you long to see all your children gathered together as one family in your love!

May this be our desire, too. Fill our hearts with the fire of your love. Give us a burning desire to share the good things you have given us, so that no one will be poor or hungry or in need of anything we can supply.

Let us find our joy in treating others' needs as our own.

Put an end to our suspicion, hatred, and divisions.

Help us to work together for a society built on justice, love, and peace.

Father, make us one family in you.

Called to compassion.

There exist also *sinful inequalities* that affect millions of men and women. These are in open contradiction of the Gospel...   (*CCC* 1938)

Reflection for Today:
No one is permitted to disregard the plight of his brothers living in dire poverty, enmeshed in ignorance, and tormented by insecurity. The Christian, moved by this sad state of affairs, should echo the words of Christ: "I have compassion on the crowd" (Mark 8:2).

Let everyone implore God the Father Almighty that the human race, which is certainly aware of these evils, will bend every effort of mind and will to their eradication. To this prayer should be added the resolute commitment of every individual.

Pope Paul VI

Father, let us share in your Son's compassion for the crowd. Give us hearts that are moved by the human sufferings displayed in the media, the streets, the places we go. Let us not be like that rich man who was so intent on feasting that he never paid attention to poor Lazarus suffering at his gate (see Luke 16:19-20). Show us what we can do to help those who suffer because of sinful inequalities in our world.

Laws that bring freedom.

The moral law is the work of divine Wisdom. Its biblical meaning can be defined as fatherly instruction, God's pedagogy. (*CCC* 1950)

Prayer for Today: Like a loving father, O God, you teach me how to live. Your fatherly counsel comes to me in so many forms—through right reason and the natural law written on my heart; through your Ten Commandments, which enlighten my conscience; and especially through the New Law of the Gospel, which comes with the grace that makes it possible for me to reach the perfection to which it calls me.

Father, how can I thank you for your law, which leads me into the true freedom of your children? Truly, my "delight is in the law of the Lord" (Psalm 1:2)!

O God of Freedom,... your laws, which you yourself have given us, are not chains—your commands are commands of freedom. In their austere and inexorable simplicity they set us free from our own dull narrowness, from the drag of our pitiful, cowardly concupiscence. They awaken in us the freedom of loving you.

Karl Rahner

Your grace is amazing, Lord!

Grace is *favor*, the *free and undeserved help* that God gives us to respond to his call to become children of God, adoptive sons, partakers of the divine nature and of eternal life. (*CCC* 1996)[31]

Prayer for Today:

O most blessed grace, which makes the poor in spirit rich in virtues, which renders him who is rich in many good things humble of heart, come, descend upon me!... If I am tempted and afflicted with many tribulations, I will fear no evils while your grace is with me.

Your grace is my strength. It will give me counsel and help. It is more powerful than all my enemies and wiser than all the wise. It is the mistress of truth, the teacher of discipline, the light of the heart, the consoler in anguish, the banisher of sorrow, the expeller of fear, the nourisher of devotion, the producer of tears. What am I without grace, but dead wood, a useless branch, fit only to be cast away?

Let your grace, therefore, go before me and follow me, O Lord, and make me always intent upon good works, through Jesus Christ, Your Son.

Thomas à Kempis

I'm a branch, not the vine.

The saints have always had a lively awareness that their merits were pure grace. (*CCC* 2011)

Prayer for Today:
"Apart from me you can do nothing" (*John* 15:5b).

Were your apostles perplexed when they first heard your words, Lord? Did it take them time to understand what it means to be as dependent on you as branches on a vine? It's certainly taking time for your words to penetrate *me!*

"I am the vine, you are the branches" (*John* 15:5).

Dear Jesus, may I abide in you as a branch on the true vine today and always, receiving your life and bearing fruit that will last.

Since whatever is good in me all comes to me from you, it is therefore more yours than mine.... Through your goodness, I have been saved by means of faith, not through any merit of mine, but through your gift; not in virtue of my works lest I become proud. I am your creature, fashioned by your grace together with my good works.

St. Augustine

God has first place.

"You shall worship the Lord your God, and him only shall you serve," says Jesus, citing *Deuteronomy* (Lk 4:8; cf. Deut. 6:13).   (*CCC* 2096)

Prayer for Today: How many masters am I serving, Lord? Help me to answer the question honestly, as I come before you for a few moments' reflection. Your Word says that "no one can serve two masters; for either he will hate the one and love the other, or he will be devoted to the one and despise the other" (Matthew 6:24).

Perhaps I've become divided in my allegiance. Perhaps the loving loyalty that rightfully belongs to you is going to other things. Perhaps I no longer worship you whole-heartedly because I've been worshiping at other altars—money, success, pleasure, fame, power.... Perhaps even very good things, like devotion to my family, have become number one over you.

My God and my all, I want to follow you! To have you is to have everything! And so if anything else is seated on the throne of my heart, I will overturn it. I will break to pieces whatever idols I discover that rival you.

Here is my heart! Do with it what you will.

Trust for the days to come.

... a sound Christian attitude consists in putting one-self confidently into the hands of Providence for what-ever concerns the future, and giving up all unhealthy curiosity about it.   (*CCC* 2115)

Reflection for Today: Why do I worry about the future and wish I could foresee it? Do I think I could handle my life more lovingly and wisely than God? Of course I couldn't! Today, I will set anxiety aside and trust in God's plan and mission for my life.

I will trust him.... If I am in sickness, my sickness may serve him; in perplexity, my perplexity may serve him; if I am in sorrow, my sorrow may serve him. My sickness, or perplexity, or sorrow may be necessary causes of some great end, which is quite beyond us. He does nothing in vain; he may prolong my life, he may shorten it; he knows what he is about. He may take away my friends, he may throw me among strangers, he may make me feel desolate, make my spirits sink, hide the future from me—still, he knows what he is about.

Cardinal John Henry Newman

Say it with reverence.

The second commandment *forbids the abuse of God's name*, i.e., every improper use of the names of God, Jesus Christ, but also of the Virgin Mary and all the saints.   (*CCC* 2146)

Reflection for Today: "Oh, I'd never commit perjury or lie under oath or blaspheme against God," I tell myself. But have I developed a tolerance for more common offenses against the second commandment?

- "Jesus Christ," a coworker mutters during a boring office meeting.
- "Holy Mary!" says a family member on opening the latest phone bill.
- "Omigod, it was so cool," a friend reports about the latest movie.

How do I react in situations like this? Do I even notice that what is holy is being trivialized? Am I myself guilty of using God's name and the names of Mary and the saints to express surprise, enthusiasm, disgust, boredom, anger?

If so, how can I change? How will I express my repentance? How can I grow in respect for God's name and for all that is holy? What will I do to promote reverence for what is holy?

In the name of the Father
and of the Son
and of the Holy Spirit. Amen.

The Christian begins his day, his prayers, and his activities with the Sign of the Cross....   (*CCC* 2157)

Prayer for Today: In a little book titled *Sacred Signs,* theologian and spiritual writer Romano Guardini encourages us to make the sign of the cross slowly, deliberately, with awareness of its power. This holiest of signs is meant to consecrate and sanctify us—mind, body, and soul—and can do so because it evokes the cross on which Christ won our salvation.

It is especially fitting, he says, to make the Sign of the Cross at particular times when we turn to God:

- before prayer: "to collect and compose ourselves and to fix our minds and hearts and wills upon God"
- after prayer: to "hold fast the gift we have received from God"
- in temptations: "to be strengthened"
- in dangers: "to be protected"
- in blessings: "that the fullness of God's life may flow into the soul and fructify and sanctify us wholly."

As we make the Sign of the Cross, let's think about these things and take the time to make it well.

Keep holy the Lord's Day.

On Sundays and other holy days of obligation, the faithful are to refrain from engaging in work or activities that hinder the worship owed to God, the joy proper to the Lord's Day, the performance of the works of mercy, and the appropriate relaxation of mind and body. (*CCC* 2185)[32]

Prayer for Today: Sunday is *your* day, Lord. A joyful day to celebrate your Resurrection and look forward to your return in glory! A day for Mass and extra prayer, for special family time and works of mercy. Thank you, Lord, for Sunday!

Sunday is the property of our good God; it is his own day, the Lord's day. He made all the days of the week: He might have kept them all; He has given you six, and has reserved only the seventh for himself. What right have you to meddle with what does not belong to you? You know very well that stolen goods never bring any profit. Nor will the day that you steal from Our Lord profit you either. I know two very certain ways of becoming poor: they are working on Sunday and taking other people's property.

St. John Vianney

About those authority figures.

According to the fourth commandment, God has willed that, after him, we should honor our parents and those whom he has vested with authority for our good. (*CCC* 2248)

Reflection for Today: Reflect on how you tend to respond to people who exercise legitimate authority over you: teachers, employers, law enforcement officials, the IRS…. Think especially about your parents, to whom you owe obedience (if you're a minor) and respect (no matter what your age, or whether or not they're still alive). Use the following verses to focus your thoughts, and end with a prayer for the "authorities" in your life.

Children, obey your parents in the Lord, for this is right. "Honor your father and mother."

EPHESIANS 6:1-2; CF. DEUTERONOMY 5:16

Remember that through your parents you were born; and what can you give back to them that equals their gift to you?

SIRACH 7:28

O son, help your father in his old age…. even if he is lacking in understanding, show forbearance; in all your strength do not despise him.

SIRACH 3:12, 13

Let every person be subject to the governing authorities. For there is no authority except from God….

ROMANS 13:1

Holy Family, help of families.

"The Christian family constitutes a specific revelation and realization of ecclesial communion, and for this reason it can and should be called a *domestic church.*"

(*CCC* 2204)[33]

Reflection for Today:

The Holy Family of Nazareth ... will not fail to help Christian families—indeed, all the families in the world—to be faithful to their day-to-day duties, to bear the cares and tribulations of life, to be open and generous to the needs of others, and to fulfill with joy the plan of God in their regard.

St. Joseph was "a just man," a tireless worker, the upright guardian of those entrusted to his care. May he always guard, protect, and enlighten families.

May the Virgin Mary, who is the Mother of the Church, also be the Mother of "the Church of the home." Thanks to her motherly aid, may each Christian family really become a "little Church" in which the mystery of the Church of Christ is mirrored and given new life....

May Christ the Lord, the Universal King, the King of Families, be present in every Christian home.... I beg of him that every family may generously make its own contribution to the coming of His Kingdom in the world.

Pope John Paul II

For civil authorities everywhere.

The Apostle exhorts us to offer prayers and thanksgiving for kings and all who exercise authority....

(*CCC* 2240)

Prayer for Today: Almighty God, hear the prayers we offer you today for all those who govern the nations of the world.

May these leaders exercise their authority as a trust and a service received from you.

May they walk in your wisdom and justice, with respect for the freedom and fundamental rights of the people entrusted them.

Inspire leaders everywhere to seek the common good and reject abuses of power.

Help them to make wise decisions and fulfill their responsibilities worthily.

May their efforts win the confidence and respect of those they govern, so that together, leaders and people may build a just society where everyone enjoys freedom, security, and peace. Amen.

...I ask that supplications, prayers, petitions, and thanksgivings be made for all men, for kings and all who are in high positions, that we may lead a quiet and tranquil life in all devotion and dignity.

1 TIMOTHY 2:1-2

To Mary, for the cause of life.

"Human life is sacred because from its beginning it involves the creative action of God and it remains for ever in a special relationship with the Creator, who is its sole end."   (*CCC* 2258)[34]

Prayer for Today:

Remember, O most gracious Virgin Mary, that never was it known that anyone who fled to your protection, implored your help, or sought your intercession was left unaided.

from St. Bernard's Memorare

O Mary, to you we come, mourning that in our world, the precious gift of human life is held so cheap.
Look down, O Mother,
on the immense multitude of babies
who are not allowed to be born,
on the sick, elderly, or handicapped people
who die because of
someone else's misguided mercy or neglect,
on all who choose to end their own lives,
on all victims of violence, overt and hidden.

Mother of mercy, to you we entrust the cause of life. Obtain for us the grace to oppose the culture of death by building the civilization of truth and love, for the praise and glory of God, who alone is the Lord and Giver of life. Amen.

Fearfully and wonderfully made.

Life and physical health are precious gifts entrusted to us by God. We must take reasonable care of them....

(*CCC* 2288)

Prayer for Today:
O Lord,
it was you who formed my inward parts;
you knit me together in my mother's womb.
I praise you, for I am fearfully and wonderfully made.
Wonderful are your works.

PSALM 139:13-14, NRSV

The more I learn about the human body, O God, the more I stand in awe of you. What the psalmist says is true: we *are* "fearfully and wonderfully made"—and far beyond what scientists can tell us!

Today, Lord, I thank you for the body you have given me. I may not like everything about it. Parts of it may fail me sometimes. Still, it is an intricate, complex, wonderfully loving gift.

Help me to care for my body in the right spirit, neither idolizing it nor harming it through neglect, thrill-seeking, or substance abuse of any kind. May I not shrink from beneficial or necessary bodily disciplines and sacrifices. May I always treat my body in a way that brings glory to you and takes account of others' needs.

Be angry, sin not.

By recalling the commandment, "You shall not kill" (Mt 5:21), our Lord asked for peace of heart and denounced murderous anger and hatred as immoral.

(*CCC* 2302)

Reflection for Today: Do I struggle with revenge and nurture grudges and angry thoughts? Have I asked the Prince of Peace to help me make peace?

Now do not think that anger is nothing.... What then is anger? The lust for vengeance. And what is hatred? Inveterate anger.... What was anger when it was new became hatred when it was turned into long continuance....

"Whoever hates his brother is a murderer" (1 John 3:15). You have not drawn the sword, nor inflicted any bodily wound, nor by any blow killed another. But the thought of hatred is in your heart, and hereby you are held to be a murderer....

Reform then, and amend yourselves. If scorpions or adders were in your houses, how you would toil to purify them, that you might dwell in safety! Yet inveterate anger is in your hearts, and there grow so many hatreds,... so many vipers. And will you not, then, purify the house of God, your heart?

St. Augustine

Peace on earth.

"Insofar as men are sinners, the threat of war hangs over them and will so continue until Christ comes again; but insofar as they can vanquish sin by coming together in charity, violence itself will be vanquished...." *(CCC 2317)*[35]

Prayer for the Day: "Peace I leave with you; my peace I give to you" (John 14:27).

Let us ... pray with all fervor for this peace which our divine Redeemer came to bring. May he banish from the souls of men whatever might endanger peace. May he transform all men into witnesses of truth, justice, and brotherly love. May he illumine with his light the minds of rulers, so that, besides caring for the proper material welfare of their peoples, they may also guarantee them the fairest gift of true peace.

Finally, may Christ inflame the desires of all men to break through the barriers which divide them, to strengthen the bonds of mutual love, to learn to understand one another, and to pardon those who have done them wrong. Through his power and inspiration may all peoples welcome each other to their hearts as brothers, and may the peace they long for ever flower and ever reign among them.

Pope John XXIII

We have put on Christ.

All Christ's faithful are called to lead a chaste life in keeping with their particular states of life. (*CCC* 2348)

Prayer for Today:
"How can a young man"—or anyone—"keep his way pure" (Psalm 119:9)?

Thank you, Lord, for giving me a way through Baptism, when I "put on Christ" (Galatians 3:27). Now I live in Jesus, who is the model of all chaste living. Through all the seasons of my life, Lord, let my appreciation and understanding of chastity flourish!

Chastity is the joyous affirmation of someone who knows how to live self-giving, free from any form of self-centered slavery.... The chaste person is not self-centered, not involved in selfish relationships with other people. Chastity makes the personality harmonious. It matures it and fills it with inner peace. This purity of mind and body helps develop true self-respect and at the same time makes one capable of respecting others....

Pontifical Council for the Family

Fighting for chastity.

Chastity … includes an apprenticeship in self-mastery.
(*CCC* 2395)

Reflection for Today: Good spiritual writers are honest about the difficulty of rooting out the self-love that leads to sin, and realistic in their practical advice. Here are two examples to ponder:

We must be in no way surprised to find self-love in us, for it never leaves us. It sleeps sometimes, like a fox, then all of a sudden leaps on the chickens. We must constantly keep watch on it and patiently and very quietly defend ourselves.

St. Francis de Sales

Let us guard against reasoning with temptations contrary to chastity. Let us try to banish them instantly—not directly, through acts of the will, but indirectly, through acts of love of God or contrition, or at least by turning our minds elsewhere….

It is most useful to turn to Jesus Christ and the divine Mother by instantly invoking them and continuing to invoke them until the temptation is beaten down. How powerful are the most holy names of Jesus and Mary against the attacks of impurity!

St. Alphonsus Liguori

Together in God, for life.

The Sacrament of Matrimony enables man and woman to enter into Christ's fidelity for his Church. Through conjugal chastity, they bear witness to this mystery before the world. (*CCC* 2365)

Prayer for Today: Spend a few minutes thinking of the married couples on whom you especially want to ask God's blessing: those whose life together has inspired you, those who are struggling, those who have asked for prayers, those who are newly married or engaged, you and your spouse (if you're married).... In your own words, or using the following prayer as a starter, ask God to make each of these unions an image of his covenant faithfulness to his people.

Father, I bring all these couples to you.
You have joined them in the sacrament of marriage: let nothing break that bond.
Strengthen what is weak in their relationship;
heal what is sick;
give abundant growth to what is good.
Keep these husbands and wives one in you, and make them one in love for each other. Show them how to help one another to holiness, so that their marriages may mirror more and more clearly Christ's own love for the Church.

Your face I seek.

The "pure in heart" are promised that they will see God face to face and be like him (cf. 1 Cor 13:12; 1 Jn 3:2). Purity of heart is the precondition of the vision of God. Even now it enables us to see *according to God*.... (*CCC* 2519)

Reflection for Today:
St. Augustine linked the spiritual gift of understanding with this Beatitude of a pure heart. The Holy Spirit wants to give us insight far beyond our own natural powers of perception. As we come to know the mind of God, we become less governed by the flesh, less oblivious to others, less preoccupied with monetary gain, less naïve, less selfish, less judgmental....

We also gradually come to see "with a cleansed eye" what eye has not seen, nor ear heard, nor has entered into the heart of man—the kingdom of God.

Benedict J. Groeschel

O God, I ask you for an understanding heart, a "cleansed eye," and the incomparable joy of gazing on you for all eternity.

A return to modesty.

Modesty protects the mystery of persons and their love. It encourages patience and moderation in loving relationships.... Modesty is decency. It inspires one's choice of clothing. It keeps silence or reserve where there is evident risk of unhealthy curiosity. It is discreet.

(*CCC* 2522)

Prayer for Today: You know well, Lord, that I live in a world that gives scant thought to modesty. It's a world where no fashion is too risqué, no topic too private to expose. A media culture of talk shows and sensational newspapers, of movie magazines and gossip columns that pry and try to appeal to the voyeur in us all. And this indecent exposure of bodies, feelings, and intimate things— well, you know, Lord, I'm affected by it too.

Take me in hand, then, and teach me how to guard my eyes and ears and tongue, how to protect what is intimate, maintain appropriate reserve, and focus on what ennobles.

Whatever is true, whatever is honorable, whatever is just, whatever is pure, whatever is lovely, whatever is gracious, if there is any excellence, if there is anything worthy of praise, think about these things.

PHILIPPIANS 4:8

Approach creation with reverence and praise.

Man's dominion over inanimate and other living beings granted by the Creator is not absolute…. it requires a religious respect for the integrity of creation.

(*CCC* 2415)[36]

Prayer for Today:

Most high, omnipotent good Lord, yours are the
praises, the glory, the honor, and all blessing.

Praised be you, my Lord, with all your creatures,
especially Sir Brother Sun,
who makes the day and illumines us through you.
And he is beautiful and radiant with great splendor
and bears your likeness, Most High One.

Praised be you, my Lord, for Sister Moon and the stars,
in heaven you formed them clear and precious and
beautiful.

Praised be you, my Lord, for Sister Water,
which is very useful and humble and precious and
chaste.
Praised be you, my Lord, for our Sister Mother Earth,
who sustains and governs us and produces varied fruits
with colored flowers and herbs.

Praise and bless my Lord and give him thanks,
and serve him with great humility.

St. Francis of Assisi, "Canticle of the Sun"

Patron of workers, pray for us.

Work can be a means of sanctification and a way of animating earthly realities with the Spirit of Christ.

(CCC 2427)

Prayer for Today:

Glorious St. Joseph, model of all those who are devoted to labor, obtain for me the grace to work in a spirit of penance for the expiation of my many sins; to work conscientiously, putting the call of duty above my inclinations; to work with gratitude and joy, considering it an honor to employ and develop, by means of labor, the gifts received from God; to work with order, peace, moderation, and patience, never recoiling before weariness or difficulties; to work above all with purity of intention and with detachment from self, having always death before my eyes and the account which I must render of time lost, of talents wasted, of good omitted, and of vain complacency in success, so fatal to the work of God.

All for Jesus, all for Mary, all after your example, O patriarch Joseph. Such shall be my watchword in life and death. Amen.

St. Pius X

Open hearts and purses.

"Not to enable the poor to share in our goods is to steal from them and deprive them of life. The goods we possess are not ours, but theirs."

St. John Chrysostom (CCC 2446)[37]

Prayer for Today: O God, you who love the poor and bless those who come to their aid, assist me in giving freely and generously of what you have given me. May I see myself as your steward and never be ensnared by love of wealth.

Christians, don't ever believe you have done enough. Christians, don't ever look upon the person who implores you to aid the poor as bothersome. Christians, have your eyes and hearts, your time and purses disposed for the great material and temporal necessities that surround you. Christians, don't make of poverty a dismal profession of lazy beggarhood; don't make of charity a source of doubtful profit. Christians, remember the beatitude that Saint Paul adds to those of the Gospel, words that come from the lips of Christ: "It is more blessed to give than to receive" (Acts 20:35).

Christians, learn how to store up treasures for eternal life by doing good here on earth.

Giovanni Battista Montini
(later Pope Paul VI)

Serving Jesus in disguise.

"When we serve the poor and the sick, we serve Jesus. We must not fail to help our neighbors, because in them we serve Jesus."

St. Rose of Lima (*CCC* 2449)[38]

Prayer for Today: "How can you see Christ in people?"...

It is an act of faith, constantly repeated. It is an act of love, resulting from an act of faith. It is an act of hope, that we can awaken these same acts in their hearts, too, with the help of God, and the works of mercy....

The mystery of the poor is this: That they are Jesus, and what you do for them you do for him. It is the only way we have of knowing and believing in our love. The mystery of poverty is that by sharing in it, making ourselves poor in giving to others, we increase our knowledge of and belief in love.   *Dorothy Day*

In what ways am I showing my love for God by assisting others?

Am I practicing the *spiritual works of mercy?*
- instructing,
- advising,
- consoling,
- comforting,
- forgiving,
- bearing wrongs patiently.

continued on next page

Am I practicing the *corporal works of mercy?*
- providing food, shelter, clothing;
- visiting the sick and imprisoned;
- burying the dead.

Take heed: beware greed.

The tenth commandment forbids *greed* and the desire to amass earthly goods without limit.   (*CCC* 2536)

Prayer for Today:
And he told them a parable, saying, "The land of a rich man brought forth plentifully; and he thought to himself, 'What shall I do, for I have nowhere to store my crops?' And he said, 'I will do this: I will pull down my barns, and build larger ones; and there I will store all my grain and my goods. And I will say to my soul, Soul, you have ample goods laid up for many years; take your ease, eat, drink, be merry.' But God said to him, 'Fool! This night your soul is required of you....' So is he who lays up treasure for himself, and is not rich toward God."

LUKE 12:16-21

Why doesn't this rich man thank God for his bounty and consider how to share it with others? He lives as though God and neighbor did not exist, isolated in his greed. Am I at all like him?

Greed takes many forms. Where am I most susceptible? Am I stockpiling anything over and above my needs? How can I become "rich toward God"?

You shall not envy.

"… rejoice in your brother's progress and you will immediately give glory to God. Because his servant could conquer envy by rejoicing in the merits of others, God will be praised."

St. John Chrysostom (CCC 2540)[39]

Prayer for Today: For St. Augustine and other spiritual writers, envy is *"the* diabolical sin."[40] The Curé of Ars warned against it, pointing out its origin in Satan's sin of pride:

Why do we envy the happiness and the goods of others? Because we are proud; we should like to be the sole possessors of talents, riches, of the esteem and love of all the world! We hate our equals, because they are our equals; our inferiors, from the fear that they may equal us; our superiors, because they are above us. In the same way, my children, that the devil after his fall felt, and still feels, extreme anger at seeing us the heirs of the glory of the good God, so the envious man feels sadness at seeing the spiritual and temporal prosperity of his neighbor.

We walk, my children, in the footsteps of the devil.

St. John Vianney

They fought the good fight.

The Christian is not to "be ashamed of testifying to our Lord" (2 Tim 1:8) in deed and word. Martyrdom is the supreme witness given to the truth of the faith.

(CCC 2506)

Prayer for Today:
Jesus, King of martyrs,
you are every martyr's inspiration and example.
Thank you for laying down your life on the cross and loving us to the end.

Jesus, King of martyrs,
you strengthened those who loved you in life so that they could follow you in your death.
We praise you for making your power perfect in human weakness.

Jesus, King of martyrs,
you give your people courage to shed their blood in proclaiming your death and resurrection.
Strengthen us to bear life's little martyrdoms courageously and to witness to you by our words and deeds.....

May we share in their triumph in your heavenly kingdom.
Amen.

Watching what we say.

... the purpose of speech is to communicate known truth to others. (*CCC* 2485)

Prayer for Today: "The tongue is a fire ... a restless evil, full of deadly poison" (James 3:6, 8). Surely not *my* tongue, Lord! But in the searching light of your truth, I must admit that I *don't* always make good use of my God-given ability to communicate. I abuse your gift through misuses of speech: flattery ... boasting ... gossip ... disparaging remarks ... "little white lies" ... bigger lies....

I repent, Lord. I want to change. I want to work for the God of all truth, not the father of lies. With your help, I will make my tongue an instrument for truth.

Man tames the wild beast, yet he does not tame his tongue. He tames the lion, yet he does not bridle his own speech. He tames everything else, yet he does not tame himself. He tames what he was afraid of; and what he ought to be afraid of, in order that he may tame himself—that he does not fear.

St. Augustine

Tame that TV ... boom box ... computer...!

Users should practice moderation and discipline in their approach to the mass media. They will want to form enlightened and correct consciences the more easily to resist unwholesome influences. (*CCC* 2496)

Reflection for Today:
"They will want to form enlightened and correct consciences...." Yes, but will *I* want to? Conscience formation is hard work—a discipline that lasts a lifetime. It means no more sitting passively in front of the tube. No more swallowing "facts" uncritically. No more unnecessarily exposing my mind and senses to media forces that dull my conscience, undermine my moral standards, and coarsen my reactions.

Oh dear. I kind of *like* being a lazy couch potato sometimes. But do I want to be a mindless sponge? A lemming who follows the crowd and meets a disastrous end?

Lord Jesus, I do not! I want to follow you. Teach me to value truth, integrity, charity, decency, humility—to give a wholehearted yes to St. Paul's directive: "Do not be conformed to this world but be transformed by the renewal of your mind, that you may prove what is the will of God, what is good and acceptable and perfect" (Romans 12:2).

Lord, We Pray

The truths of the faith figure as part of each Christian's "vital and personal relationship with the living and true God. This relationship is prayer" (*CCC* 2558). Part four of the *Catechism*, "Christian Prayer," deals with this crucial reality—one that has immediate relevance for anyone who is using a book like *Praying the Catechism!*

"For me, prayer is a surge of the heart," wrote St. Thérèse of Lisieux (*CCC* 2558)[41]. For us as we begin this section, this "surge of the heart" means praying about issues related to prayer. We will contemplate Jesus as our chief model and intercessor, and the Holy Spirit as our teacher and guide. We will meditatively explore types and sources of prayer—God's word, the liturgy, the virtues of faith, hope, and charity—as well as helps and hindrances to our conversation with God.

This might be a good time to get better acquainted with two prayers that are highlighted in this section of the *Catechism*. The first is actually a collection of prayers, the Psalms: "Prayed by Christ and fulfilled in him, the Psalms remain essential to the prayer of the Church" (*CCC* 2586)[42].

Not surprisingly, the second prayer highlighted in this

section is the prayer that has been called "the summary of the whole gospel,"[43] "the most perfect of prayers,"[44] and "the quintessential prayer of the Church" (*CCC* 2761; 2763; 2776): the "Our Father." You already know the Lord's Prayer. Now try praying it as so many saints and spiritual writers recommend: slowly, meditatively, letting each word penetrate and transform.

Chosen, called, and cherished.

In prayer, the faithful God's initiative of love always comes first; our own first step is always a response.

(*CCC* 2567)

Prayer for Today: "You did not choose me, but I chose you" (John 15:16). Loving God, when I think of these words of Jesus to the apostles at the Last Supper, I'm reminded that not just the Twelve but every one of your Son's followers has been specially chosen. Me included!

Even before I knew of you, you were calling me, preparing the path by which I could approach you. Every time I pray, I come drawn by your own love and longing, which then well up in me. I may put energy and effort into seeking you, but you seek me first and give me the grace to respond.

How wonderful is your love, O my God!

Our prayer is God's work, God's creation. As you kneel there, sit there, walk about or whatever you do when you pray, you are saying "Yes" with your whole being to his will that you should be, that you should be you, that you should be united to him.

Maria Boulding

Open my lips, Lord.

Prayed and fulfilled in Christ, the Psalms are an essential and permanent element of the prayer of the Church. (*CCC* 2597)

Reflection for Today: Have you ever considered getting better acquainted with the psalms by praying the Liturgy of the Hours? The Divine Office, as it is also called, is the Church's official prayer and is offered at specified times of the day by priests and religious. If you're not already joining in, as many lay Catholics do, you might think about doing so to begin or end your day.

Psalms are the backbone of the Liturgy of the Hours—a treasury of timeless prayers for every mood and circumstance. Not only that: the psalms are the prayers that Jesus prayed during his earthly life (see, for example, Mark 14:26; 15:34).

Still more amazing: in the Liturgy of the Hours, Jesus prays them still. When we join in, as Vatican II explained, we offer "the very prayer which Christ himself together with his Body addresses to the Father."

Lord, open my lips.
And my mouth will proclaim your praise.

PSALM 51:15
(*This verse opens each day's Liturgy of the Hours.*)

At the foot of the cross.

When the hour had come for him to fulfill the Father's plan of love, Jesus allows a glimpse of the boundless depth of his filial prayer ... even in his *last words* on the Cross.... (*CCC* 2605)

Reflection for Today: Choose one of Jesus' "seven last words" to reflect on. If you can, consult your Bible to remind yourself of the context. Picture the scene, and place yourself mentally at the foot of the Cross. Ponder Jesus' words in silence, letting them penetrate you. Then speak to Jesus from the heart.

"Father, forgive them; for they know not what they do" (Luke 23:34).

"Truly, I say to you, today you will be with me in Paradise" (Luke 23:43).

"Woman, behold your son!".... "Behold your mother!" (John 19:26-27).

"I thirst" (John 19:28).

"My God, my God, why have you forsaken me?" (Mark 15:34, NRSV; cf. Psalm 22:1).

"It is finished" (John 19:30).

"Father, into your hands I commit my spirit!" (Luke 23:46, NRSV).

Hold fast.

[The parable of] "the importunate widow" (cf. Lk 18:1-8) is centered on one of the qualities of prayer: it is necessary to pray always without ceasing and with the *patience* of faith. (*CCC* 2613)

Prayer for Today: Lady, you didn't stand a chance to win that lawsuit. You had a good case. And the law of the land was supposed to favor defenseless widows. But your judge was corrupt. "I neither fear God nor regard man," he crowed (Luke 18:4). He hadn't reckoned with your scrappy tenacity, though!

Father, I don't have to fight to get your attention and make my case. You are a just Judge who always hears me when I pray. May I become as persistent as this widow and her real-life counterpart, the Canaanite woman whose faith Jesus praised (see Matthew 15:21-28).

One must hold fast to prayer and never give it up. In this game, the one who lets it go loses everything. If it seems that no one is listening to you, cry out all the louder. If, like the Canaanite woman, you are told that you do not deserve the grace you are asking for, affirm like her that you expect no unusual favors, but only hope to eat the crumbs that fall from the divine table.

St. Jane de Chantal

We praise and adore you!

Adoration ... exalts the greatness of the Lord who made us (cf. Ps 95:1-6) and the almighty power of the Savior who sets us free from evil.   (*CCC* 2628)

Prayer for Today:

> O come, let us sing to the Lord;
> let us make a joyful noise to the rock of our
>   salvation!
> Let us come into his presence with thanksgiving;
> let us make a joyful noise to him with songs of praise!
> For the Lord is a great God,
> and a great King above all gods.
> In his hand are the depths of the earth;
> the heights of the mountains are his also.
> The sea is his, for he made it;
> for his hands formed the dry land.
> O come, let us worship and bow down,
> let us kneel before the Lord, our Maker!

PSALM 95:1-6

Teach me to see the mystery of your majesty. Let me be aware that my being is fulfilled when it bows before you.

Romano Guardini

First abide. Then ask.

The first movement of the prayer of petition is *asking forgiveness*, like the tax collector in the parable: "God, be merciful to me a sinner!" (Lk 18:13). (*CCC* 2631)

Prayer for Today:
Dear Father, do I approach you in the right spirit?
I'd like to think I do.
I like to see myself as the tax collector
    humbly imploring your mercy.
How offensive that Pharisee is—
    so convinced he stands head and shoulders
    above other people,
    so full of pride at his fasting and tithing.
"Thanks, God, for having made me such a fine person.
    And don't forget all I'm doing for you."
The nerve!
No, I'm not like him.
Am I, Father?

Holy Spirit, shine your purifying light into my heart. Tell me: where is the Pharisee alive in me? In what areas is my pride keeping me from abiding in you? With the psalmist and the tax collector, I can only pray, "Have mercy on me, O God" (Psalm 51:1).

"If you abide in me, and my words abide in you, ask whatever you will, and it shall be done for you."
JOHN 15:7

146

Looking to others' needs.

Since Abraham, intercession—asking on behalf of another—has been characteristic of a heart attuned to God's mercy.   (*CCC* 2635)

Prayer for Today: Compassion for the welfare of others moved Abraham to intercede with God for the people of Sodom (see Genesis 18:22-33). "Mind your own business," God could have said. "Don't argue with me." Instead, he let Abraham bargain, and he agreed to spare the city if only ten just men could be found in it.

Just God, we thank you that you are more inclined to mercy than to severity. We thank you that you desire the salvation of sinners—of whom we are the first—and not their death.

We thank you too for calling us to share in your mercy through our prayers of intercession for others' needs, especially their spiritual needs. We present those needs to you now. (*Take a few minutes to mention the people you want to pray for.*)

Father, we offer our prayer through Jesus, our eternal high priest, who stands at your right hand "to save those who draw near to God through him, since he always lives to make intercession for them" (Hebrews 7:25). Amen.

Rejoice—always?

Every joy and suffering, every event and need can become the matter for thanksgiving which, sharing in that of Christ, should fill one's whole life: "Give thanks in all circumstances" (1 Thess 5:18).   (*CCC* 2648)

Reflection for Today: How successful are you at "always and for everything giving thanks" (Ephesians 5:20)? Do you remember to thank God for small blessings, or do you tend to accept them unthinkingly? Do major joys move you to readily acknowledge their Giver?

What about sufferings big and small? Would joyful thanks come more easily if you had absolute trust that "in everything God works for good with those who love him" (Romans 8:28)?

Be grateful for the smallest gift and you will be worthy to receive a greater. Value the least gift as much as the greatest, the simplest as much as the most special. If you consider the dignity of the Giver, no gift will appear too small or worthless. Even if he gives punishments and pains, accept them gladly, for God always acts for our welfare in whatever he allows to befall us.

Thomas à Kempis

Remember, wonder, and praise!

Praise ... lauds God for his own sake and gives him glory, quite beyond what he does, but simply because HE IS. (*CCC* 2639)

Prayer for Today: Holy Triune God, you are worthy of all praise! I praise you for your infinite greatness, and I praise you too for the saving deeds by which I glimpse that greatness. May I never forget what you have done for me and for all your people. May my remembering lead me to that perfect praise of awesome wonder at who you are!

Praise the Lord!
Praise God in his sanctuary;
praise him in his mighty firmament!
Praise him for his mighty deeds;
praise him according to his exceeding greatness!

Praise him with trumpet sound;
praise him with lute and harp!
Praise him with timbrel and dance;
praise him with strings and pipe!
Praise him with sounding cymbals;
praise him with loud clashing cymbals!
Let everything that breathes praise the Lord!
Praise the Lord!

PSALM 150

Speak, Lord, I'm listening.

"... prayer should accompany the reading of Sacred Scripture, so that a dialogue takes place between God and man." *(CCC* 2653)[45]

Prayer for Today: Holy Spirit, please keep me mindful of the fact that I mustn't read Scripture in the way I read other books. Never let me open your word without praying, "Lord, please speak to me." And when you do speak, may I listen actively and attentively, always ready to learn and obey.

The knowledge of Scripture is knowledge of Christ and his teaching. One time Jacques Maritain spoke to us in a little dingy church hall in the Italian section of New York, a hall which was dirty and cold and smelling of beer.... [He] spoke simply of the love of God and especially of the need to study the Scriptures in order to find Christ, him whom our soul loves. "Read the Gospel prayerfully," he said, "searching for the truth, and not just to find something with which to back up your own arguments," he added with humor.

Dorothy Day

We are liturgical creatures.

Prayer internalizes and assimilates the liturgy during and after its celebration.   (*CCC* 2655)

Prayer for Today: Christ Jesus, Anointed One, we thank you for the liturgy—for the Eucharist and for all the sacramental celebrations that make the mystery of your dying and rising present to us. As you address your prayer to the Father in the Holy Spirit, you allow us to share in your priesthood. We participate in this great "work of God" and are rooted and grounded in the love of the Trinity.

Christ Jesus, help us to experience the liturgy as the center of life and ourselves as liturgical creatures made for heavenly worship. May the saving mysteries in which we participate nourish our personal prayer. And through our personal prayer, may the effects of this public worship transform how we live and make every other part of our lives the liturgy *after* the liturgy.

The liturgy is the summit toward which the activity of the Church is directed; it is also the font from which all her power flows.

Constitution on the Sacred Liturgy

Love draws us on.

Love is the source of prayer; whoever draws from it reaches the summit of prayer. (*CCC* 2658)

Prayer for Today: May we "know the love of Christ which surpasses knowledge," that we "may be filled with all the fullness of God" (Ephesians 3:19). May our hearts burn with love for him to whom we pray.

I feel so much love upon my soul; it is like an ocean into which I plunge and lose myself. It is my vision on earth, while I await the vision face to face in the Light. He is in me and I am in him. I have only to love him, to let myself be loved, at all times, in all circumstances. To awake in love, to move in love, to sleep in love, my soul in his soul, my heart in his Heart, that I may be delivered and purified from my miseries by contact with him.

Blessed Elizabeth of the Trinity

Embracing the present.

...time is in the Father's hands; it is in the present that we encounter him, not yesterday nor tomorrow, but today... (*CCC* 2659)

Prayer for Today: I bring my wandering thoughts before you, Father. Keep me from squandering my time—*your* time—in useless dwelling on the past, planning the future, lingering in daydreams. I entrust my past to your mercy, my future to your Providence. I will seek to accomplish your will in the only segment of time I possess: the present.

O Father, the first rule of our dear Savior's life was to do your will. Let his will of the present moment be the first rule of our daily life and work, with no other desire but for its most full and complete accomplishment. Help us to follow it faithfully so that, doing what you wish, we will be pleasing to you.

St. Elizabeth Seton

Just as a traveler in a train would not think of moving forward through the cars so as to get to his destination sooner, but remains seated and lets the train carry him along, so our souls, to get to God, should fulfill wholeheartedly his will in the present moment, since time moves forward on its own.

Chiara Lubich

The Name above all other names.

To pray "Jesus" is to invoke him and to call him within us. His name is the only one that contains the presence it signifies.   (*CCC* 2666)

Reflection for Today: "Lord Jesus Christ, Son of God, have mercy on me, a sinner." Try praying this "Jesus Prayer" often as you go about your routine today. You will be joining in with the chorus of needy but faith-filled people who have been crying out to Jesus ever since Gospel days (see Matthew 9:27; 15:22; 20:29; Mark 10:47; Luke 17:13; 18:13, 38).

Derived from "the name ... above every name" (Philippians 2:9), the prayer may be compressed into one word: "Jesus." With this one powerful word, we throw ourselves open to God's mercy and invite the Lord of love and life to make his home in us.

When I invoke the name of Jesus ... I am drawn into his name, immersed in his name, immersed in him.... "Jesus," the word is already a prayer.

Catherine Doherty

Behold this Heart,
which has loved you so much.

The prayer of the Church venerates and honors the *Heart of Jesus* just as it invokes his most holy name. It adores the incarnate Word and his Heart which, out of love for men, he allowed to be pierced by our sins.

(*CCC* 2669)

Prayer for Today:

Hail, Heart of my Jesus: save me!

Hail, Heart of my Creator: perfect me!

Hail, Heart of my Savior: deliver me!

Hail, Heart of my Judge: pardon me!

Hail, Heart of my Father: govern me!

Hail, Heart of my Master: teach me!

Hail, Heart of my King: crown me!

Hail, Heart of my Benefactor: enrich me!

Hail, Heart of my Pastor: guard me!

Hail, Heart of my Brother: stay with me!

Hail, Heart of incomparable goodness: have mercy on me!

Hail, most loving Heart: set me on fire with your love!

St. Margaret Mary

Sacred Heart of Jesus, let me love you and make you loved.

Best of Teachers, teach us to pray.

The Holy Spirit, whose anointing permeates our whole being, is the interior Master of Christian prayer.

(*CCC* 2672)

Prayer for Today:

"No one can say 'Jesus is Lord!' except by the Holy Spirit" (1 Corinthians 12:3). *Come, Holy Spirit!*

"The Spirit helps us in our weakness; for we do not know how to pray as we ought, but the Spirit himself intercedes for us with sighs too deep for words. And he who searches the hearts of men knows what is the mind of the Spirit, because the Spirit intercedes for the saints according to the will of God" (Romans 8:26-27). *Come, Holy Spirit!*

"If you, then, who are evil, know how to give good gifts to your children, how much more will the heavenly Father give the Holy Spirit to those who ask him!" (Luke 11:13). *Come, Holy Spirit!*

"And I will pray the Father, and he will give you another Counselor, to be with you for ever" (John 14:16). *Come, Holy Spirit!*

To Mary, Star of the Sea.

Like the beloved disciple we welcome Jesus' mother into our homes (cf. Jn 19:27), for she has become the mother of all the living. We can pray with and to her.
(*CCC* 2679)

Reflection for Today:
When the winds of temptations rise up, when you run up against the rock of tribulation, look at the star, cry out to Mary. When you're tossed by waves of pride or ambition or slander or jealousy, look at the star, cry out to Mary. When anger or greed or sexual desires batter the ship of your soul, look to Mary.... When you start sinking into the depths of sadness or the abyss of despair, think of Mary. In dangers, in anguish, in every doubt, think of Mary, cry out to Mary. May her name never be far from your lips, may she never leave your heart.

If you seek the help of her prayers, imitate the example of her life. Following her, you will never go astray. Praying to her, you will never become discouraged. Keeping her in your thoughts, you will never wander away. With your hand in hers, you will not fall; under her protection, you will not fear. Led by her, you will not grow weary. With her help, you will reach your goal.

St. Bernard of Clairvaux

Tilling our soil.

Ordained ministers, the consecrated life, catechesis, prayer groups, and "spiritual direction" ensure assistance within the Church in the practice of prayer.

(*CCC* 2695)

Prayer for Today: Jesus told the following parable to illustrate the range of responses to the word of God. Read it slowly, with your prayer life in mind. Afterwards, ask yourself a few questions:

What kind of soil am I?

Am I doing what I can to cultivate my "soil" through prayer?

Could I benefit from someone's help?

"Listen! A sower went out to sow. And as he sowed, some seed fell along the path, and the birds came and devoured it. Other seed fell on rocky ground, where it had not much soil, and immediately it sprang up, since it had no depth of soil; and when the sun rose it was scorched, and since it had no root it withered away. Other seed fell among thorns and the thorns grew up and choked it, and it yielded no grain. And other seeds fell into good soil and brought forth grain, growing up and increasing and yielding thirtyfold and sixtyfold and a hundredfold." And he said, "He who has ears to hear, let him hear."

MARK 4:3-9

At home for God.

"We must remember God more often than we draw breath" (*St. Gregory of Nazianzus*).[46] But we cannot pray "at all times" if we do not pray at specific times, consciously willing it. (*CCC* 2697)

Prayer for Today:
How will I come to love you more, dear God, if I don't come to know you better?
And how will I know you if I don't seek your company?
You stand at my door and knock, but I'm not always at home to receive you.
I'm too busy about other things, not serious enough about the one thing needful.

Forgive me, Lord, for leaving you on the doorstep.
Help me to put out my welcome sign: to pray regularly, so that I can always be at home when you come.

Most welcome Guest,
to you I fling open the door of my heart!

When I see what patience God has had with me....
May his Majesty no longer allow me to have the power to offend him the least bit; rather, may I be consumed in this prayer.

St. Teresa of Avila

Lift up your voice.

Vocal prayer is an essential element of the Christian life.
(*CCC* 2701)

Prayer for Today:

Hear, O Lord, when I cry aloud, be gracious to me
and answer me!

PSALM 27:7

I will bless the Lord at all times;
his praise shall continually be in my mouth.
My soul makes its boast in the Lord;
let the afflicted hear and be glad.
O magnify the Lord with me,
and let us exalt his name together!

PSALM 34:1-3

Hear my voice, O God, in my complaint!

PSALM 64:1

I cry with my voice to the Lord,
with my voice I make supplication to the Lord,
I pour out my complaint before him,
I tell my trouble before him.

PSALM 142:1-2

Thank you, God for giving me a voice with which to
praise you, bless you, beseech you, thank you—and yes,
even complain to you!

Ecce Homo.

Meditation engages thought, imagination, emotion, and desire…. Christian prayer tries above all to meditate on the mysteries of Christ…. (*CCC* 2708)

Prayer for Today: Meditating on the sufferings that Jesus underwent for us is one time-honored way of growing in devotion. "All the saints have learned the art of loving God from the study of the crucifix," said St. Alphonsus Liguori. Which scenes from Christ's Passion do you find especially rich for meditation?

I tried to picture Christ within me, and I used to find myself getting the most benefit from thinking of those mysteries of his life during which he was most lonely. In particular, I used to feel most at home when I accompanied him as he prayed in the Garden of Gethsemane. I thought of the bloody sweat and agony he endured there. I wished it were possible for me to wipe the sweat from his face, but I remember that I never dared to do it: my sins seemed to me too grievous….

For many years, nearly every night before I fell asleep,… I always used to think a little of this mystery of the prayer in the Garden…. I believe that my soul gained a great deal in this way.

St. Teresa of Avila

The gaze of faith.

"Contemplative prayer … in my opinion is nothing else than a close sharing between friends; it means taking time frequently to be alone with him who we know loves us."

St. Teresa of Avila (*CCC* 2709)[47]

Prayer for Today:

How unworthy I am to gaze upon you, Lord, you who are so glorious in majesty.

Who can see your face and live?

Yet with confidence inspired by your love, I dare to pray: "Your face, Lord, I seek. Don't hide your face from me" (see Psalm 27:8-9).

Place your mind before the mirror of eternity!
Place your soul in the brilliance of glory!
Place your heart in the figure of the divine substance!
And transform your whole being into the image
of the Godhead Itself through contemplation!
So that you too may feel what his friends feel
as they taste the hidden sweetness
which God himself has reserved
from the beginning for those who love him.

St. Clare of Assisi

Incompatible? Think again.

Many Christians unconsciously regard prayer as an occupation that is incompatible with all the other things they have to do.... (*CCC* 2726)

Prayer for Today: This fourth-century exhortation about the relevance of Scripture is a helpful reminder about our need for prayer in general:

I'm always encouraging you—and I'm not going to stop encouraging you!—to keep on reading sacred Scripture. And don't let anyone say to me ... "I'm stuck at the courthouse all day," "I'm tied up with political affairs," "I'm in an apprenticeship program," "I've got a wife," "I'm raising kids," "I'm responsible for a household," "I'm a businessman. Reading the Bible isn't my thing."

What are you saying, man? It's not your business to pay attention to the Bible because you're distracted by thousands of concerns? Then Bible reading belongs especially to you. You're always standing in the line of battle, you're constantly being hit, so you need more medicine than other people. For not only does your wife irritate you, but your son annoys you, and a servant makes you lose your temper.... Often a lawsuit impends, poverty distresses, loss of possessions brings sorrow.

A thousand missiles rain down on us from every direction. And so we constantly need the whole range of equipment supplied by Scripture.

St. John Chrysostom

Those pesky, revealing distractions.

The habitual difficulty in prayer is *distraction*.

(*CCC* 2729)

Prayer for Today:
Why, O Lord, is it so hard for me to keep my heart directed toward you? Why do the many little things I want to do, and the many people I know, keep crowding my mind...? Why does my mind wander off in so many directions...? Are you not enough for me?

Henri Nouwen

Perhaps I'm afraid, Lord. Perhaps I'm scared that as I open myself to you, I'll discover uncomfortable things about myself. My heart needs purifying, I know: my distractions prove it. Help me let go, Lord, and surrender fully to you.

All good prayer is based on honest self-knowledge, and it is painful for us to confront ourselves honestly.... The desire for quiet is very real, but when the time comes that I am free, how difficult it can be to really focus the leisure, to confront myself and the Lord honestly and deeply.

Thomas H. Green

Keeping love alive in dry times.

Dryness belongs to contemplative prayer when the heart is separated from God, with no taste for thoughts, memories, and feelings, even spiritual ones. This is the moment of sheer faith clinging faithfully to Jesus in his agony and in his tomb.   (*CCC* 2731)

Prayer for Today:
O God, you are my God, I seek you,
my soul thirsts for you,
my flesh faints for you,
as in a dry and weary land
where there is no water.

Psalm 63:1, NRSV

In times of aridity when I am incapable of praying, of practicing virtue, I seek little opportunities, mere trifles, to give pleasure to Jesus; for instance a smile, a pleasant word when inclined to be silent and to show weariness. If I find no opportunities, I at least tell him again and again that I love him; that is not difficult and it keeps alive the fire of love in my heart. Even though this fire of love might seem to be extinct I would still throw little straws upon the embers and I am certain it would rekindle.

St. Thérèse of Lisieux

Draw me after you.

The most common yet most hidden temptation is our *lack of faith* ... our lack of faith reveals that we do not yet share in the disposition of a humble heart: "Apart from me, you can do *nothing*" (Jn 15:5). (*CCC* 2732)

Prayer for Today: "Draw me after you," says the bride to the bridegroom in the Song of Songs (1:4)—a request which St. Bernard interpreted as the wise soul's plea to Jesus:

> The bride has great need to be drawn onward, and drawn by no other than he who says, "Without me you can do nothing" (John 15:5)....
>
> She knows that your ways are blessed and that anyone who follows you does not walk in darkness. But if she prays to be drawn onward, it is because she cannot attain to your righteousness on her own strength. She prays ... because no one comes to you unless the Father draws him (John 6:44)....
>
> When, therefore, you feel sluggish, lukewarm, and weary, do not give way to unbelief or stop your spiritual practices, but seek the hand of him who can help you. Beg like the bride to be drawn, until you are reawakened and reinvigorated by grace.
>
> *St. Bernard of Clairvaux*

Speak to me of hope.

The humble are not surprised by their distress; it leads them to trust more, to hold fast in constancy.

(*CCC* 2733)

Prayer for Today:
My God, speak to me of hope....

You forbid me ever to become discouraged at the sight of my misery and to tell myself: "I can't go any further. The road to heaven is too narrow...."

You forbid me to look at my faults—those faults for which I ask your forgiveness every day and into which I fall back endlessly—and to tell myself: "I'll never be able to improve. Holiness isn't for me...."

You forbid me to look at the infinite graces you have showered on me and at the unworthiness of my present life and to tell myself: "I haven't made good use of so many graces. I should be a saint, and I'm a sinner. After all God has done, there's nothing good in me. I'll never get to heaven."

You want me to hope in spite of everything.

Heaven and me, this perfection and my wretched state—whatever can these things have in common?

Your Heart, my Lord Jesus. Your Heart creates the link between two things that are so unlike.

Charles de Foucauld

Wait and trust.

"Do not be troubled if you do not immediately receive from God what you ask him; for he desires to do something even greater for you, while you cling to him in prayer."

Evagrius Ponticus (*CCC* 2737)[48]

Reflection for Today: Unanswered prayer—is there any in your life? Is there any request you've been bringing to God for a long time—for something very dear to your heart—that you haven't yet seen fulfilled?

Do you think your prayer is in line with God's will for the situation? Are you asking with the right motives? How can you know? Have you told God, "not my will but yours"?

Do you firmly believe that God is trustworthy and that he has your best interests at heart? Tell him what you think. If you can, make an act of trust.

Sometimes it seems that we have been praying a long time and still do not have what we ask. But we should not be sad. I am sure that what our Lord means is that either we should wait for a better time, or more grace, or a better gift.

Julian of Norwich

Asking for the best.

If our prayer is resolutely united with that of Jesus, in trust and boldness as children, we obtain all that we ask in his name, even more than any particular thing: the Holy Spirit himself, who contains all gifts.

(CCC 2741)

Prayer for Today: Father, let me know the holy boldness of the apostles and the Christians of the early Church who cried out to you in the name of your Son—that name at which "every knee should bow, in heaven and on earth and under the earth, and every tongue confess that Jesus Christ is Lord, to the glory of God the Father" (Philippians 2:10-11).

Let me know with them the joy of receiving the best of your gifts: "And when they had prayed, the place in which they were gathered together was shaken; and they were all filled with the Holy Spirit and spoke the word of God with boldness" (Acts 4:31).

Heavenly King, Comforter,
Spirit of Truth,
You are everywhere present and fill all things.
Treasury of blessings and Giver of life,
Come and dwell within us.
Cleanse us of all stain,
and save our souls,
O gracious Lord.   *Byzantine Liturgy*

Prayer is a battle.

Against our dullness and laziness, the battle of prayer is that of humble, trusting, and persevering *love*.

(*CCC* 2742)

Prayer for Today:

My God, how far I am from acting according to what I know so well! I confess it, my heart goes after shadows. I love anything better than communion with you. I am ever eager to get away from you. Often I find it difficult even to say my prayers. There is hardly any amusement I would not rather take up than set myself to think of you. Give me grace, O my Father, to be utterly ashamed of my own reluctance! Rouse me from sloth and coldness and make me desire you with my whole heart. Teach me to love meditation, sacred reading, and prayer. Teach me to love that which must engage my mind for all eternity.

Cardinal John Henry Newman

Lord, you know all things: you know I love you. But you also know how fickle and unfocused I can be. Help me as I struggle to approach you in prayer. Defend me against the wiles of Satan, who seeks to keep me from you. Draw me through love, and I will run to you!

Pray as you work.

"It is possible to offer fervent prayer even while walking in public or strolling alone, or seated in your shop,… while buying or selling,… or even while cooking."

St. John Chrysostom (2743)[49]

Prayer for Today: One teacher of this art is a seventeenth-century French Carmelite, Brother Lawrence. In his *Practice of the Presence of God*, the lay brother explained how he enjoyed God's presence even while serving as monastery cook:

"I turn my little omelette in the pan for the love of God; when it is finished, … I adore my God, who gave me the grace to make it."

Whether you're turning an omelette, driving a bus, balancing accounts, or drilling teeth today, you too can find God on the job.

In order to be with God throughout the day, it is not necessary to stay in church all the time. We can make our heart like a little chapel into which we retire from time to time to converse with him gently, humbly, and lovingly. Everyone is capable of these familiar conversations with God—some more, others less. Our Father knows what we can do. Let us begin. Perhaps he is only waiting for a generous resolution on our part.

Brother Lawrence of the Resurrection

What Jesus prayed for us.

When "his hour" came, Jesus prayed to the Father (cf. Jn 17).... Christian Tradition rightly calls this prayer the "priestly" prayer of Jesus.   (*CCC* 2746; 2747)

Reflection for Today: Ponder these verses in which Jesus prays for us, who believe in him through the testimony of others:

> "I do not pray for these only, but also for those who believe in me through their word, that they may all be one; even as thou, Father, art in me, and I in thee, that they also may be in us, so that the world may believe that thou hast sent me.... Father, I desire that they also, whom thou hast given me, may be with me where I am, to behold my glory, which thou hast given me in thy love for me before the foundation of the world."
>
> JOHN 17:20-21, 24

Jesus, you prayed that your disciples would be as united with one another as you are with the Father. Give me a heart for unity among your people and a willingness to work for it.

Jesus, you prayed that your disciples would see you in the fullness of your glory. Let your prayer be fulfilled in me!

God is our Father.

... the Lord's Prayer *reveals us to ourselves* at the same time that it reveals the Father to us. (*CCC* 2783)[50]

Prayer for Today: Address the Creator of the universe as our Father? See ourselves as his beloved sons and daughters? Whoever could have imagined such a wondrous mystery! What does it mean for how we should live?

O Son of God! My tender Master! How is it that even from the first words of the Our Father you give us so many good things at once?... How is it that you go so far as to give us, in your Father's name, everything that can be given? For you want him to look on us as his children.... This is no small burden. If he is our Father, he is obliged to bear with us, no matter how serious our offenses. He has to forgive us when we return to him like the prodigal son. He has to comfort us in our trials, see to our sustenance—and all this in a manner that befits a Father like him, whose goodness necessarily surpasses that of all earthly fathers, because every perfection is found in him. And besides all this, he must make us sharers and heirs with you!

St. Teresa of Avila

In a multitude, but not faceless.

... if we pray the Our Father sincerely, we leave individualism behind, because the love that we receive frees us from it. (*CCC* 2792)

Prayer for Today: Father, you love me not just as one of a crowd but as an individual. You know what makes me most *me,* and you cherish my uniqueness as only my Creator can. Secure in your love, I can count myself as one of a multitude who call you Father.

Dear Father, bless all your children—my brothers and sisters in Jesus. Help us to renounce divisions and suspicions and to relate as members of one family. Increase our love for one another until, like your own love for us, it know no bounds.

Now we say Our Father all together; what all-embracing generosity! The emperor says it, the beggar says it; the slave says it, his master says it.... They must realize that they are brothers, since they all have one Father. The master must not scorn to have as a brother the slave of his whom the Lord Christ was willing to have as a brother.

St. Augustine

Heaven is within.

"Who art in heaven" does not refer to a place but to God's majesty and his presence in the hearts of the just.
(*CCC* 2802)

Reflection for Today:
You already know that God is everywhere. Well obviously, where the king is, there is his court. Therefore, wherever God is, there is heaven....

St. Augustine recounts that he sought the Lord in many places and finally found him within himself [*Confessions* 10, 27]. Do you consider it a small advantage for a person with a wandering heart to recognize this truth and to learn that there is no need to rise up to heaven to speak with one's eternal Father and find delight in him? Nor is there any need to shout in order to speak with him. However softly we speak, he will hear, he is so close. You need no wings to find him; all you have to do is go in solitude, look within, and not stray from so excellent a Guest. In all humility, speak with him as to a Father. Bring him your requests, as you would to a father; tell him about your trials and ask for help, realizing that you are not worthy to be his daughter.

St. Teresa of Avila

Guilty of blasphemy?

"… we ask that this name of God should be hallowed in us through our actions. For God's name is blessed when we live well, but is blasphemed when we live wickedly."

St. Peter Chrysologus (*CCC* 2814)[51]

Prayer for Today:
You are holy, O God,
and because you are holy,
so must your people be.
Hallowed be your name.

You warned Israel to keep and follow your commandments:
"You shall not profane my holy name," you said.
"I will be hallowed among the people of Israel;
I am the Lord who sanctify you" (Leviticus 22:32).
Hallowed be your name.

And when your people rejected your commands and profaned your holy name, you told them you would act:
"I will vindicate the holiness of my great name….
the nations will know that I am the Lord" (Ezekiel 36:23).
Hallowed be your name.

But even now, O God,
your holy name is tarnished by our sinful lives.
"The name of God is blasphemed among the Gentiles
because of you" (Romans 2:24).
Forgive us and have mercy.
Hallowed be your name.

Your Kingdom come.

... the Church looks first to Christ's return and the final coming of the Reign of God. It also prays for the growth of the Kingdom of God in the "today" of our own lives. (*CCC* 2859)

Prayer for Today:
This kingdom has not yet completely arrived among us. But each day it comes closer, little by little, and imperceptibly it extends its boundaries more and more. This happens in those whose inner self is renewed day by day, thanks to God's help. To the measure that the kingdom of grace is extended, sin's power is diminished.... But even those people who seem more perfect in this mortal state have to acknowledge that "in many things we all offend" (James 3:2).... This is why they too pray without ceasing, "May your Kingdom come."

St. Bernard of Clairvaux

Is the Kingdom coming in me, as I surrender to God's renewing action? Is the Kingdom coming in my relationships and environments, as I carry out my part in the Church's saving mission to the world?

Holy Spirit, am I hindering or helping your activity? How can I cooperate?

Your will, Father, not mine.

... united with Jesus and with the power of his Holy Spirit, we can surrender our will to him and decide to choose what his Son has always chosen: to do what is pleasing to the Father (cf. Jn 8:29). (*CCC* 2825)

Prayer for Today: "The words 'Thy will be done' must be the rule of the Christian's life in all their fullness," wrote St. Edith Stein.

What about me? Is doing the Father's will the principle by which I live? Do I trust God enough to surrender myself to his will? Can I at least want to aspire to this surrender?

My God, my Father,
I abandon myself into your hands;
do with me what you will.
Whatever you may do with me, I thank you.

I am ready for all, I accept all,
provided that your will be done in me,
in all your creatures.
I want nothing besides my God.

My love impels me to give myself to you,
to surrender myself into your hands,
without reserve
and with unlimited confidence,
for you are my Father.

Charles de Foucauld

Teach and strengthen us to do your will.

By prayer we can discern "what is the will of God" and obtain the endurance to do it (Rom 12:2; cf. Eph 5:17; cf. Heb 10:36). (*CCC* 2826)

Prayer for Today: Reflect on these Scripture verses, then respond with your own prayer or the one below.

"Be transformed by the renewal of your mind, that you may prove what is the will of God" (Romans 12:2).

"Do not be foolish, but understand what the will of the Lord is" (Ephesians 5:17).

"You have need of endurance, so that you may do the will of God and receive what is promised" (Hebrews 10:36).

O Holy Spirit, soul of my soul, I worship you.
Enlighten me, guide me,
strengthen and comfort me.
Tell me what I must do.
Give me your commands.
I promise to submit myself
to whatever you may want of me
and to accept whatever you allow to befall me.
Only let me know your will.

Cardinal Mercier

For daily needs we pray.

... Jesus insists on the filial trust that cooperates with our Father's providence.[52] He is not inviting us to idleness,[53] but wants to relieve us from nagging worry and preoccupation. (*CCC* 2830)

Prayer for Today: To one of her married daughters who was concerned about her family's material needs, St. Jane de Chantal wrote these words of advice. Can you relate?

You are too attached to the things of this life and take them too much to heart. What do you have to be afraid of?... Have no apprehensions, I beg you, for in this you wrong the providence of him who gives you your children and who is good enough and rich enough to nourish and provide for them in a way that advances his glory and their salvation....

Now, my dearest daughter, look lovingly on all these little creatures as entrusted to you by God.... Care for them, cherish them tenderly, and bring them up not in vanity but faithfully, in the fear of God.... Entrust all these anxieties to divine providence and you will see how all will be provided for.... Take my advice, dearest daughter, and throw yourself into these safe arms.

St. Jane de Chantal

Called to share our daily bread.

In the Beatitudes, "poverty" is the virtue of sharing: it calls us to communicate and share both material and spiritual goods, not by coercion but out of love, so that the abundance of some may remedy the needs of others (cf. 2 Cor 8:1-15).   (*CCC* 2833)

Prayer for Today: "For you know the grace of our Lord Jesus Christ, that though he was rich, yet for your sake he became poor, so that by his poverty you might become rich" (2 Corinthians 8:9).

Jesus, teach me what it means to embrace poverty for love of others. Fill me with your love, that I may willingly share the daily bread of my food, my goods, my time and energy, my thoughts and prayers, my very self.

The poorest man in a religious community is not necessarily the one who has the fewest objects assigned to him for his use.... Often the poorest man in the community is the one who is at everybody else's disposition. He can be used by all and never takes time to do anything special for himself.

Thomas Merton

O Living Bread come down from heaven.

"[Christ] himself is the bread who, sown in the Virgin, raised up in the flesh, kneaded in the Passion, baked in the oven of the tomb, reserved in churches, brought to altars, furnishes the faithful each day with food from heaven."

St. Peter Chrysologus (CCC 2837)[54]

Prayer for Today:

O bread of heaven! beneath this veil
you do my very God conceal.
My Jesus, dearest treasure, hail!
I love you, and adoring, kneel.
The loving soul by you is fed
with your own self in form of bread.

O food of life! you who do give
the pledge of immortality!
I live—no, it's not I that live:
God gives me life; God lives in me.
He feeds my soul, he guides my ways,
and every grief with joy repays.

Beloved Lord! in heaven above,
there Jesus, you do wait for me
to gaze on you with changeless love.
Yes, this I hope. So shall it be!
For how can he deny me heaven
who, here on earth, himself has given?

from a hymn by St. Alphonsus Liguori

As we forgive our debtors.

It is not in our power not to feel or to forget an offense; but the heart that offers itself to the Holy Spirit turns injury into compassion and purifies the memory in transforming the hurt into intercession.

(*CCC* 2843)

Prayer for Today: Jesus, how easy it is to ask your blessing on my friends. Now, with your Spirit's help, I bring before you what I desire for my enemies and for those who have injured me.

But first, merciful Lord, I ask that you yourself inspire those desires. Whatever you lead me to ask for my enemies, give it to them and give the same back to me.

Lead my enemies into your light, your truth, your love—and me along with them. Let us be reconciled to you and to one another, according to your will.

O merciful Judge,
forgive me all my debts, as I now forgive all those who are indebted to me.
I cannot do this perfectly yet.
But know, Lord, that I wish to
and that I will do all I can to forgive from the heart.

inspired by a prayer for enemies by St. Anselm

A struggling sailor's S.O.S.

When we say "lead us not into temptation" we are asking God not to allow us to take the path that leads to sin. (*CCC* 2863)

Prayer for Today:

Blessed is that person who has steered his boat straight into Paradise.

St. Ephraim the Syrian

O God, I am in distress. Come and rescue me!
My little boat is frail and threatened—
tossed and pounded by wind and waves,
pulled about by dangerous currents,
or drifting idly, sometimes, into perilous places.

Lord, I am not such a good sailor.
I am not always vigilant at the helm.
I steer my boat too close to rocks.
But you are with me in my boat!
I will listen for your voice
and will close my ears to the tempter's siren song.
Strengthen me, O Captain of my life,
and I will stay the course to the end.

My Jesus, if you do not uphold me, I shall fall.
My Jesus, if you do not help me, I am ruined.

St. Philip Neri

Deliver us from evil.

When we ask to be delivered from the Evil One, we pray as well to be freed from all evils, present, past, and future, of which he is the author or instigator.

(CCC 2854)

Reflection for Today: What is the evil from which the Our Father teaches us to ask for deliverance? The great difficulty in answering this question, says one spiritual writer, is that there are so many evils to choose from!

We do not have to make special efforts to find them; they press on us from all sides: sickness and want, sorrow, misfortune, and death. Our own experience and the knowledge of our heart incite us to turn with all our afflictions to the Lord of the world and to beg Him to help us.

Romano Guardini

Lord Jesus, Lord of the world, we do turn to you in our distress. Deliver us from every evil, especially those which are especially on our minds and which we bring before you now....

Do not let us fall prey to the evil one, who seeks our ruin and misery. You have conquered him, victorious Savior! Let us share in your triumph!

Amen. So be it.

"Then, after the prayer is over you say 'Amen,' which means 'So be it,' thus ratifying with our 'Amen' what is contained in the prayer that God has taught us."

St. Cyril of Jerusalem (*CCC* 2856)[55]

Prayer for Today: "Amen" expresses wholehearted agreement with what has just been said. It engages our will and signifies our determination to seek the Kingdom. It speaks of commitment and constancy. With our "amen," we put our lives on the line and make ourselves totally available to God, as Mary did: Amen. *Fiat.* "Let it be done to me according to your word" (Luke 1:38).

For the kingdom, the power, and the glory are yours, now and forever. Amen.

Blessed be the Lord, the God of Israel,
from everlasting to everlasting!
And let all the people say, "Amen!"
Praise the Lord!

PSALM 106:48

"Surely, I am coming soon."
Amen. Come, Lord Jesus!

REVELATION 22:20

List of Abbreviations

CA	*Centesimus annus*
CCL	Corpus Christianorum, Series Latina (Turnhout, 1953–)
CDF	Congregation for the Doctrine of the Faith
CIC	Codex Iuris Canonici
CPG	*Solemn Profession of Faith:* Credo of the People of God
DV	*Dei Verbum*
FC	*Familiaris consortio*
GILH	General Introduction to the Liturgy of the Hours
GS	*Gaudium et spes*
LG	*Lumen gentium*
PG	J.P. Migne, ed., Patrologia Graeca (Paris: 1857–1866)
PL	J.P. Migne, ed., Patrologia Latina (Paris: 1841–1855)
PO	*Presbyterorum ordinis*
SC	*Sacrosanctum concilium*
STh	*Summa Theologiae*

Notes

These notes contain the material that appears in footnotes in the original text of the Catechism.

General Introduction

1. John Paul II, Apostolic Constitution *Fidei Depositum,* paragraph 2.

2. *CCC* 2559, St. John Damascene, *De fide orth.* 3, 24: PG 94, 1089C.

Part One: Introduction

3. *CCC* 197, St. Ambrose, *Expl. Symb.* 1: PL 17, 1193.

Part One: Section 1

4. *CCC* 32, St. Augustine, *Sermo* 241, 2: PL 38, 1134.

5. *CCC* 51, DV 2; cf. *Eph* 1:9; 2:18; *2 Pet* 1:4.

6. *CCC* 127, St. Thérèse of Lisieux, *ms. autob.,* A 83v.

Part One: Section 2

7. *CCC* 230, St. Augustine, *Sermo* 52, 6, 16: PL 38:360 and *Sermo* 117, 3, 5: PL 38, 663.

8. *CCC* 336, St. Basil, *Adv. Eunomium III,* 1: PG 29, 656B.

9. *CCC* 494, St. Irenaeus, *Adv. haeres.* 3, 22, 4: PG 7/1, 959A.

10. *CCC* 766, Cf. St. Ambrose, *In. Luc.* 2, 85-89: PL 15, 1666-1668.

11. *CCC* 795, St. Augustine, *In Jo. ev.* 21, 8: PL 35, 1568.
12. *CCC* 825, *LG* 11 § 3.
13. *CCC* 888, *PO* 4.
14. *CCC* 901, *LG* 34; cf. *LG* 10.
15. *CCC* 947, St. Thomas Aquinas, *Symb.* 10.
16. *CCC* 975, Paul VI, *CPG* § 15.
17. *CCC* 991, Tertullian, *De. res.* 1,1: PL 2, 841.
18. *CCC* 1032, St. John Chrysostom, *Hom. in Cor.* 41, 5: PG 61, 361; cf. *Job* 1:5.

Part Two: Section 1

19. *CCC* 1067, *SC* 5 § 2.
20. *CCC* 1090, *SC* 8; cf *LG* 50.

Part Two: Section 2

21. *CCC* 1217, *Roman Missal,* Easter Vigil 42: Blessing of Water.
22. *CCC* 1296, *2 Cor* 1:21-22; cf. *Eph* 1:13; 4, 30; Cf. Revelation 7:2-3; 9:4; Ezekiel 9:4-6.
23. *CCC* 1458, St. Augustine, *In Jo. ev.* 12, 13: PL 35, 1491.
24. *CCC* 1513, Cf. CIC, can. 847 § 1.
25. St. John Vianney, quoted in B. Nodet, *Jean-Marie Vianney, Curé d'Ars.* 100.
26. *CCC* 1603, *GS* 48 § 1.
27. *CCC* 1652, *GS* 50 § 1.

Part Three: Section 1

28. *CCC* 1821, St. Teresa of Avila, *Excl.* 15:3.
29. *CCC* 1863, St. Augustine, *In ep. Jo.* 1, 6: PL 35, 1982.
30. *CCC* 1896, Cf. *CA* 3, 5.
31. *CCC* 1996, Cf. *Jn* 1:12-18; 17:3; *Rom* 8:14-17; *2 Pet* 1:3-4.

Part Three: Section 2

32. *CCC* 2185, Cf. CIC, can. 1247.
33. *CCC* 2204, *FC* 21; cf. *LG* 11.
34. *CCC* 2258, CDF, instructions, *Donum vitae,* intro. 5.
35. *CCC* 2317, *GS* 78 § 6.
36. *CCC* 2415, Cf. *CA* 37-38.
37. *CCC* 2446, St. John Chrysostom, *Hom. in Lazaro* 2, 5: PG 48, 992.
38. *CCC* 2449, P. Hansen, *Vita mirabilis* (Louvain, 1668).
39. *CCC* 2540, St. John Chrysostom, *Hom. in Rom.* 71, 5: PG 60, 448.
40. *CCC* 2539, Cf. St. Augustine, *De catechizandis rudibus* 4, 8: PL 40, 315-316.

Part Four: Introduction

41. *CCC* 2558, St. Thérèse of Lisieux, *Manuscrits autobiographiques,* C 25r.
42. *CCC* 2586, Cf. GILH, nn. 100-109.
43. *CCC* 2761, Tertullian, *De orat.* 1: PL 1, 1155.
44. *CCC* 2763, St. Thomas Aquinas, *STh* II-II, 83, 9.

Part Four: Section 1

45. *CCC* 2653, *DV* 25.

46. *CCC* 2697, St. Gregory of Nazianzus, *Orat. theo.*, 27, 1, 4: PG 36, 16.

47. *CCC* 2709, St. Teresa of Jesus, *The Book of Her Life*, 8, 5 in *The Collected Works of St. Teresa of Avila*, tr. K. Kavanaugh, OCD, and O. Rodriguez, OCD (Washington, DC: Institute of Carmelite Studies, 1976), I, 67.

48. *CCC* 2737, Evagrius Ponticus, *De oratione* 34: PG 79, 1173.

49. *CCC* 2743, St. John Chrysostom, *Ecloga de oratione* 2: PG 63, 585.

Part Four: Section 2

50. *CCC* 2783, Cf. *GS* 22 § 1.

51. *CCC* 2814, St. Peter Chrysologus, *Sermo* 71, 4: PL 52:402A.

52. *CCC* 2830, Cf. *Mt* 6:25-34.

53. *CCC* 2830, Cf. *2 Thess* 3:6-13.

54. *CCC* 2837, St. Peter Chrysologus, *Sermo* 67: PL 52, 392; cf. *Jn* 6:51.

55. *CCC* 2856, St. Cyril of Jerusalem, *Catech. myst.* 5, 18: PG 33, 1124; cf. *Lk* 1:38.